THROUGH
The
EYES OF GOD

The Essentials Of Building Your Life According To God's Plan

BERNARD O. APPIAH, PHD

ISBN: 978-9988-2-1383-1

For enquiries contact the author:
Email: otopah01@yahoo.co.uk
Tel: 00 44 7572 612 947

Printed in the UK.
Lightning Source (UK) Ltd

Chapter House

Pitfield

Kiln Farm

Milton Keynes,

Buckinghamshire

MK11 3LW,
United Kingdom

Ingram Content Group

1 Ingram Blvd

La Vergne, TN 37086

United States

Lightning Source Australia PTY Ltd.

1246 Heil Quaker Blvd

Unit A1/A3 7Janine Street VIC 3179
Australia

Design: *Print Innovation (printinnovationghana@gmail.com)*

Dedication

Lady Julie- my wife, my lover, my friend, my confidante, you are the great pillar in my building.
Chrystabel Nhyiraba, Faith Aseda, Leon Nyameye, you make me feel like the most blessed one on earth, I couldn't have better kids like you.
Thanks for your understanding, sacrifices and love that compel me to build meticulously recognizing you are depending on me, it is very much appreciated.

Aknowledgements

Mr William & Mrs Selina Amoah, it is true 'there is a friend that sticks closer than a brother' you are that kind of friends.

My Sisters and my brothers-in-law – Anita & Kofi, Pearl & Dickson, indeed blood is thicker than water! Thanks for your unflinching support.

Introduction

For which of you, intending to build a tower, does not sit down first and count the cost, whether he has enough to finish it— lest, after he has laid the foundation, and is not able to finish, all who see it begin to mock him, saying, 'This man began to build and was not able to finish'?Luke 14:28-30

You Have A Life To Build

The Life of humans has been studied since the beginning of civilisation in the context of different disciplines, which includes philosophy, psychology, sociology, biology, religion and many more. Consequently, the precise description of life is one that has caused a lot of controversy over the years with differing views due to its complex nature. The differing views on the precise description of life have resulted from the individual's or group's orientation based on the discipline through which the subject has been studied or investigated.

However, there is one universal fact that can be accepted by all, and that is; humans have a role to play in developing or building their lives. In the scripture quotation above, Jesus used the analogy of building a tower to illustrate the importance of preceding any venture with adequate preparation. Furthermore, revealing the fact of the role, we have to play in building our lives. Moreover, anyone who builds must first know what they want to build (intending to build a tower), assess and analyses not only the magnitude of the job (sit down first and count the cost) to be done but also whether (whether he has enough to finish it) they personally have what it takes to finish. The most important thing is to finish what you begin to build.

Nevertheless, understanding the broader conceptual framework of the life you want to build is essential. This is the concept that life is a system.

Life Is a System

We can liken the building and development process of a human life in many respects to the construction of a building. From getting the architectural designs to land preparation, to the laying of the foundation, to putting up the frame to roofing, through to securing windows and doors to the finish. All parts of a building are important and should be made to fit with each other. This should be done to match it to the architectural dimensions shown on the plan. Each part and stage has its own functions, combining with others to produce a meaningful architectural piece. A building in itself is a system and so is life.

A system is an entity that maintains its existence and functions as a whole through the interaction of its parts[1]. We work in organizations that have adopted the use of systems thinking and tools to guide change in organizations[2], but we may have never thought of applying it to our lives, to help us build the stable, adaptable and happy life we are seeking. There is no way we can live our lives without appreciating the fact that our life is a system. We may not have much difficulty in accepting that the body is a system and yet find it difficult to embrace the fact that life does not end with the body. The human life is made up of the spirit, the soul and the body. These constituent parts make it a system. The human life being a system means that it has three main stages; the inputting stage, the processing stage and outputting stage. This happens with our voluntary or involuntary involvement. In spite of the fact, we may not know or be conscious of these stages does not exonerate us from the blame or praise of the output.

The difficulty sometimes, in viewing life from this perspective is partly because we sometimes shudder at the responsibility we have if we have to produce anything significant with it. Therefore, like the proverbial ostrich, we bury our heads in the sand to pretend nothing is happening around us, although the happenings around us affect us. On the other hand, we sometimes make the mistake of viewing or analysing life from a traditional perspective. This focuses on separating the individual pieces or breaking up life into constituent parts instead of expanding our view to take into account larger and larger numbers of interactions between the constituents (spirit, soul and body).

As part of the construction process, builders encounter obstacles that they have to deal with in order to proceed to the subsequent stages. Additionally, when the building has been finished, there is no longer the burden to build but rather to maintain. Every one of these stages is of the highest importance to say the least. Therefore, a subtraction of any stage of the construction process by the builder will produce something that falls short of a building or even cause serious structural problems for the other stages as some precede others in a systematic fashion. For instance, one cannot put up the frame of a building without first, having a foundation to sit on.

This is because the behaviour of a system would depend on how the parts are related. In other words, the way a system behaves is due to how every one of the inter-related parts function. What do I mean? A pile of bricks is not a system. If you remove a brick, you still have a pile of bricks. Nevertheless, a functioning car is a system. Remove the fan belt and you no longer have a working car. In the same way, eliminate any of the constituent parts (spirit, soul and body) of the human, and you do not have a life.

In the analogy of life being a building, it is the parts and the process of bringing each of them together through the stages and the interaction they have with each other that makes the building what it is. Therefore to have a beautiful building, is to have beautiful parts painstakingly brought together exactly as it appears on the plan. With these in place, we deal with parts, which have problems or develop problems, to improve the overall stability, beauty and even the value of the building. Similarly, the output of a person's life is heavily dependent on the input and the processes they go through. The input may embody the ideologies, information, truths and realism and so on, by which the individual lives. The processes involve the application of these philosophies, information, self-knowledge, realism and so on to our day-to-day life experiences. Consequently, the output is what a person's life turns out to be because of the input and processes the individual go through.

In an instance where an individual is underachieving in life all the various parts of his or her life would have to be examined to ascertain where the problem has occurred and then a solution be sought for the part with the problem. That is not the end; we need to make adjustments with other parts to fit very well with the part repaired in order to extend its margins of stability, durability and functionality not disregarding the aesthetics.

The Paradigm of the Life System

From the perspective of the paradigm postulated by this book, if a man or woman is under achieving - which is an equivalent of failing to manifest the design of the architect it may be because he or she has not put the foundation in place generally, or has a defect in a specific area of one of its constituents. As we may find in this book for example, the foundation for everything in life has already been laid. There is no need for a re-engineering, as this foundation is Jesus Christ. To have Jesus Christ in your life and continue to align your value systems to His and the Kingdom of God becomes the definitive factor of having the right foundation to under gird your efforts for building a solid life.

Life is less incomprehensible when viewed from the perspective described above. This paradigm of the life system is an answer to the question of how one can build a solid life holistically through the examination of the parts that makes life what it is when brought together. In the centre of this paradigm is the paradoxical reality that the builder is also at the same time the building. Like a building, a life must have a foundation, a frame, a roof among others and the builder must have a mechanism for dealing with obstacles to the progress of the building process as well as develop a maintenance culture. All these must be applied within the framework established by the supreme architect who is God. It is to this end that many stories, anecdotes, illustrations and time-tested principles have been drawn from scripture and pieced together to enlighten the reader on how to meet the structural demands of the construction process.

The Result of Embracing this Paradigm

Maybe you are reading this book, and you are thinking whether it is the right one for you due to your age and accumulated experience in life. H. L. Mencken, notes that "The older I grow the more I distrust the familiar doctrine that age brings wisdom." Whatever stage you are in your life's development and building process, this book comes as a framework for benchmarking, as it is part of a larger effort to encourage a process of re-engineering and or a quality improvement initiative of your life. Through this, you would find the basis to discover what you are about on this planet and what the architect expects of you as a builder. You will also find the need to pay particular attention to your core competencies or capabilities and find scenarios, illustrations and life stories of people confronted with the middle (obstacles) as well, and how they handled it as part of the life building process, and how to sustain your accomplishments and many more. Concisely, this book provides you with the indicators of the materials you need at the various stages and the outcome to expect.

What I hope this book will bring about in your life is a fundamental systemic change of the traditional, humanistic life building programs and principles to a holistic approach that incorporates spirituality. These principles originate from Holy Scripture, and conveyed from a heart of a man who wants to see the world changed through the maturing of its peoples into graceful leaders.

It is a sheer understatement to say we can all live a meaningful happy life, if our lives are well constructed, appropriating rightly the principle presented herein. Join me on this expedition of life building as we embrace this paradigm of the life system to build a solid life by practicing the timeless principles herein.

CONTENTS

PART
O N E

Turning Intention into a Preparation to Build

Before anything else, preparation is the key to success.

Alexander Graham Bell

1

Preparation on the Backdrop of the Architect's Plan in Mind

The only true happiness comes from squandering ourselves for a purpose. - **William Cowper**

Seek to Find the Plan and Design of the Architect

We have all come into this world under different circumstances, some in wedlock, some out of wedlock, some were abandoned on garbage dumps, and some were dumped by riverbanks in inclement weather. Whatever the circumstances that surrounded your birth, you are not on earth by accident. Firstly, God is the one who formed you and knows you, and secondly He has a purpose for your being on this planet for this moment in time. Ancient

Greek philosophers noticed that all living creatures are designed to pursue a certain goal. Every species has a different goal. They called this goal "telos" which means "end." They taught us that, if you can discover what something's telos (final goal) is, then you would know what that creature is. For example, the goal of an acorn is "oak tree." Acorns already have "oak tree" written within their nature. In the same way, if we can discover the "end" or "goal" of the human being, we will know what the human being is.[3]

The scripture below, is a dialogue between God and Jeremiah, this principle is not exclusive to Jeremiah but to all humankind.

Then the word of the LORD came to me, saying:

"Before I formed you in the womb I knew you;

Before you were born, I sanctified you;

I ordained you a prophet to the nations."

Then said I: "Ah, Lord GOD!

Behold, I cannot speak, for I am a youth."

But the LORD said to me:

"Do not say, 'I am a youth,'

For you shall go to all to whom I send you,

And whatever I command you, you shall speak.

(Jeremiah 1:4-7)

Jeremiah's expression of self-doubt was because he was too young to carry out God's mandate. God's response was that he knew Jeremiah, even before he was born into this world. In other words, He knew him too well to make a mistake to mismatch him to a job. Because He formed Jeremiah, He knew the abilities He had placed in him and therefore could not require of Jeremiah something beyond him. There are times that due to difficult circumstances and a few failed endeavours; we feel we are here to struggle to find out what we can do with our lives. As a result, some feel they are alone. These thoughts and imaginations dampen our spirits, steal our enthusiasm quietly from us, and make us susceptible to self-pity. However, that is not right because God knows you, and He is with you. When a sparrow falls from the sky, He sees it. It is impossible for him to forget all about you. He knows the number of hairs on your head (Matthew 10:30).

You Are Not an Accident

Furthermore, in Ecclesiastes 3:1 God says, "To everything there is a season, a time for every purpose under heaven:" God declares through His Word, there is a purpose for everything. God planned your life even before you came here on earth. He has a blue print for your life, a reason for your existence. It was the same as found in the story of the prophet

Jeremiah. God ordained him as a prophet to the nations. This means that Jeremiah would not have succeeded in any other vocation or profession if he had ignored God's call. God ordained him to prophesy. This is exactly what He (God) has done for every human being born into this life. Every one is born to do something specific in life. No one is born unexpectedly into this world irrespective of the means by which we arrived here. God has a plan and a design for your life and the onus is on you to find it and live your life according to it. Life ceases to be a struggle when you discover the architect's (God) design for your life. Can you imagine spending so much money buying your building materials and going ahead to get a builder to build your house, not looking at the plan and the architectural drawings? Definitely, the builder would erect a structure but the chances are that, it would not fit the design of the architect. Under this circumstance, the architect may ask for the demolition of the whole structure because what is on the plan and for which the building permission has been given by the appropriate agency, is different from what exists in reality. Discover the purpose for your existence now.

Tips to Discover The Purpose Of Your Existence

We need to find out the purpose for our existence, to enable us build according to the plan and design provided by the architect. We do not choose what we want to be and neither do we stumble into it; we need to consult the architect to reveal to us what we are supposed to build. You can discover or find out the plan by:

1: Praying and seeking Him for a precise word about His blueprint for your life.

2: Finding out what make you happy. There are things that will make you happy in life but one makes you feel extremely happy. Usually one of those things is tied to your purpose. As life, goes on this may change a little as well as develop into something much bigger.

3: Looking at what you are good doing. It is so easy to overlook what we are good at because we tend to focus on what areas we want to improve. However, there is at least one thing that just comes naturally to you. What you are naturally gifted at will usually be a part of your purpose. Just because you may not have, a talent that someone else has does not mean that you do not have talent. Your gifts make you unique and help define your purpose in life. The gifts themselves are not the purpose to be fulfilled; they are the tools with which the purpose is to be fulfilled.

4: Do it! 'Do not think to do, just do it'. I think this point is so important. People expend years and years thinking about what their purpose is and end up doing nothing with their life but just thinking. On the other hand, people that are not certain of what their purpose is but just get out there start doing things that they enjoy. Beforehand, they have turn out to be very successful and are fulfilling part of their purpose.

5: Identifying who inspires you most. Anyone you know or do not know. It could be someone from your family, a friend, an author, an artiste, a leader, etc.

Which qualities inspire you, in each person? If you answer these questions accurately, the answers should be an indication of what you are meant to be and to do that will bring you much fulfilment.

6: What were some challenges, difficulties and hardships you have overcome in the past or are in the process of overcoming? How did you do it? Most times God calls a person back to help deliver others from what He has delivered him or her.

These indicators may not be exhaustive but lucid enough to help you discover the Architect's (God) plan for your life. You may have commenced building already, but you can choose to find out whether you are building according to the plan and design supplied by the architect. This will bring you great fulfilment.

Build to the Architect's Specification

God is particular about building according to specification.

'And let them make Me a sanctuary, that I may dwell among them. According to all that I show you, that is, the pattern of the tabernacle and the pattern of all its furnishings, just so you shall make it'. (Exodus 25:8-9)

The above scriptural reference is a classic example of God requiring that Moses build the tabernacle according to the pattern that He will show him. Anything other than what God showed Moses in the mountain would not have been appropriate for His tabernacle. Seek for the architect's design and build your life according to it.

After you have discovered your reason for living, this would then form the basis of certain important decisions you make in your lifetime; as to the career you choose, the kind of education you put yourself through and so on. All these things should help you to fulfil the contents of the architect's design for your life. When you discover God's purpose for your life, you will begin to appreciate your personality, gifts, talents, abilities and potential. You will understand why you are what you are because you are meant to use those as tools to etch out your design. You will begin to love yourself more because you can understand why you are what you are, even in appearance.

It is simply not enough to discover the plan for your life but to build according to it.

Do Not Let Us Down

When you discover what the architect's plan and design is, you will not chase after fame or look for a moment to make you famous. If you concentrate to build according to the design of the architect, you will be famous in your own right. You will be amazing in your field. Bear in mind that the purpose God has given you is unique and outstanding. The purpose you have to fulfil is unique and no one else can do it, the way you will. This is partly the reason why you must build according to the plan and design of the architect instead of just building anything; you must build according to the plan and design of the architect. Your refusal to commit fully to fulfil your purpose would deprive others of what they need as part of their building. If you consider the analogy used in the scripture below; (1Corinthians 12:12-21) all humans are inter dependent to the extent that we all suffer if one person refuses to be who The Creator has made him or her to be.

For as the body is one and has many members, but all the members of that one body, being many, are one body, so also is Christ. For by one Spirit we were all baptized into one body—whether Jews or Greeks, whether slaves or free—and have all been made to drink into one Spirit. For in fact the body is not one member but many. If the foot should say, "Because I am not a hand, I am not of the body," is it therefore not of the body? And if the ear should say, "Because I am not an eye, I am not of the body," is it therefore not of the body? If the whole body were an eye, where would be the hearing? If the whole were hearing, where would be the smelling? But now God has set the members, each one of them, in the body just as He pleased. And if they were all one member, where would the body be? But now indeed there are many members, yet one body. And the eye cannot say to the hand, "I have no need of you"; nor again the head to the feet, "I have no need of you." (1 Corinthians 12:12-21)

Do not let the rest of us down. Someone is waiting on the fulfilment of your purpose as an input for the fulfilment of his or her own. Arise and be counted as one of the people that fulfilled their purpose, the design of the architect.

Prepare the Grounds

It is equally important to prepare the grounds for the building in the same way, as you would seek to know what the architect's plan and design are. In putting up physical buildings, the preparation of the grounds or the process of land preparation before builders erects a structure may include clearing up the land of weeds, levelling the ground to give an appropriate gradient for building. Builders make demarcations and place pegs in the exact spot the intended structure is expected to be. This is only a few of many technical details of how the builders prepare the grounds for constructing a building.

On the other hand, in life building, the ground preparation may involve, educating yourself, developing excellence, developing the passion to build, creating a mental picture of the desired results, clearing up space and putting in the landmarks. Let us look at each of the above-mentioned preparatory activities in much detail.

Educate Yourself

This may not necessarily be undertaking a formal education but a way of getting the right information about what you are supposed to build and doing it to the delight of the architect and reading this scriptural based book is one of them. In our day of DIY (Do It Yourself), many people can assemble complex equipments, which before now were carried out by a trade's men for a fee. This has become possible because information manuals are included in the product sold. We would stretch the meaning of education in this sense to mean gaining maturity and good judgement that becomes an asset in the building process. Malcolm Forbes has once said, "Education's purpose is to replace an empty mind with an open one." Jesus Christ for instance was never heard of from the age of twelve until about thirty when His ministry began as shown in the scripture verses below.

Then He went down with them and came to Nazareth, and was subject to them, but His mother kept all these things in her heart. Furthermore, Jesus increased in wisdom and stature and in favour with God and men. (Luke 2:51-52)

Some bible scholars believe from the above that Jesus submitted himself to His parents to grow and mature in preparation for His mission and purpose during this time. It is true that if you have full knowledge and understanding of what your purpose is in life, you can forge ahead.

In addition, gather facts and information about people who have built their lives according to the architect's plan and design successfully. Allow them to mentor you into maturity so you can build your life successfully. Mentoring can take many forms apart from having a personal relationship with your mentor. It could simply include following the ideologies or philosophy that under girds the life of the mentor. With the world fast becoming a global village using information technology based accesses, you can easily find a mentor to follow. The exciting thing about mentoring is that you do not need to experience what they have learnt through tears and pains; you get the experience through their stories. Largely, it helps you to avoid certain pitfalls and watch out for the things that would help you to build successfully.

Guidelines To Choosing A Good Mentor

Here are a few general tips to guide you to choose a mentor. The application of the points discussed below should not be taken exclusively to having a personal relationship with the mentor. It may depend on one's circumstances. Follow the steps below.

Step 1: The very first thing you should do is to make a catalogue of the people you would like to be your mentor/mentors. Do not be fearful to put names on your list. You have nothing to lose except for the pluck to accept the word no with gracefulness. Bear also in mind that God fulfils the desire of our hearts, and so it is possible to have some of the names on the list willing to mentor you.

Step 2: At this moment in time, there are individuals whom you would never think of asking to mentor you considering that you are afraid they might say no. Not withstanding, you will be amazed to find out how people are enthusiastic to share their recipe for accomplishment if they are asked.

Step 3: Please, ask courteously and politely. Do not feel like anyone is beholden to help you. No one truly has plenty of spare time unoccupied to share with you. Mentoring others require sacrifice. It is a decision to deprive one's self of other commitments in order to be with you. Moreover, that is valuable.

Step 4: Would you go to a barrister about your migraine? I doubt it. Why then do some of us go to people who are not living our dream for advice? You need people with transferable expertises and knowledge you can use. The objective is not to search for advice from a teacher but somewhat from a doer.

Nothing is further disastrous than taking counsel from someone who has a concealed plan. There are persons who feel easy giving you advice as long as you are subordinate to them. In the near future, as you step up one rung of the ladder in front of them, they get envious. They may not express verbally or own up to this, but you will feel it. So, make sure you know the person cares about you. It is for this reason you have to involve God for His direction to identify the right person to contact.

Get yourself educated

Having expressed the need for some form of informal education is not a way of dismissing formal education. Indeed if for instance you are to become a caterer, you may need to go to college, or enrol on an apprenticeship. Therefore, all together, whether formal or informal, education is essential to prepare for the building. Anatole France once said, "An education isn't how much you have committed to memory, or even how much you know. It's being able to differentiate between what you do know and what you don't." When you discover what you do not know, you should find a way to know it. Those who seek surely find.

Develop Excellence

The quality of excellence must be seen in the life we are building, by so doing God can be proud about us and make us an example to the world. Actually, for those who believe in Jehovah God or believers, excellence is no longer an option but a mandate and an obligation. This is so because excellence identifies us with the one to whom we belong.

But you are a chosen generation, a royal priesthood, a holy nation, His own special people, that you may proclaim the praises of Him who called you out of darkness into His marvelous light; 10 who once were not a people but are now the people of God, who had not obtained mercy but now have obtained mercy. (1Peter 2:9-10)

From the scripture above, the reason, why God chose believers for himself and made them royal priesthood, special people, and a holy nation is so that they would show forth His praises. The original Greek word translated as praises in the New Testament has other renderings that include "imminent qualities" and "excellencies". In other words, the believer should live so that their heavenly Father's qualities are conspicuous in their lives. We can probe the rendering "excellent or Excellencies" a bit more. In ancient Greek, this word was used to describe adept sports men, women, and political leaders. In the case of sports when a person had come up tops in an athletic event. They can then say the person is excellent because he or she surpasses all competitors, and has been outstanding. In other words, he or she stands out of many. It is for a similar reason that those who have stood for an election and won the mandate of the people to govern as head of the country, are referred to as His or Her Excellency. To talk about being outstanding, means that you went beyond where most people would stop. God requires us to have His qualities, and demonstrate it in our lives. Through Jesus Christ, God has shown His imminent qualities of excellence.

Develop The God-kind Of Excellence

Then God said, "Let there be light"; and there was light. And God saw the light, that it was good; and God divided the light from the darkness. God called the light Day, and the darkness He called Night. So the evening and the morning were the first day.

Genesis 1:3-5

The effort to build our lives according to the plan and design of the architect would be excellent, if we do it exactly as He has made known to us as He did in the verses from the Book of Genesis above. The reason is that God is an exemplification of flawlessness and cannot be surpassed in this regard. Look at how the mountains and the rocks are arranged, the stars of the skies, the vast oceans, these points to Him as the perfect designer. The Excellency of God is also expressed in the way He reviewed what He did after each day and concluded it was good. To ensure what we build is according to the plan, we need to do a frequent review as part of every stage of the building process as God did.

However, we can reach out to be as excellent as He is. This journey towards developing excellence begins when we submit our lives to Him. He becomes the gauge of our actions and all we do. Hence, when God comes to live in you as you believe in Him, He comes with all His imminent qualities and attributes of which excellence is one of them. Michael J Fox is quoted in Lorne A. Adrian's "The Most important Thing I know" as saying, "I am careful not to confuse excellence with perfection. Excellence, I can reach for; perfection is God's business." We can all aspire to do everything with excellence because it makes us look more like our creator.

Excellence Makes You Stand Out

It is important to note that we are not building to please ourselves but God whose design, we need to build as He has shown to us.

It pleased Darius to set over the kingdom one hundred and twenty satraps, to be over the whole kingdom; and over these, three governors, of whom Daniel was one, that the satraps might give account to them, so that the king would suffer no loss. Then this Daniel distinguished himself above the governors and satraps, because an excellent spirit was in him; and the king gave thought to setting him over the whole realm. (Daniel 6:1-3)

Daniel was chosen for a high office because an excellent spirit was in him. The excellent spirit distinguished him from the rest of the administrators and governors. It is most likely this attitude transcended the entire life of Daniel and not only in his job as governor. The Hebrew word rendered as excellent in the verse already quoted, means "outstanding, exceedingly, exceptional"[4]. When this meaning is applied, it presupposes that Daniel's job and everything else he did was exceptional and outstanding. It stood out of the crowd; it was first in the line of many. If men could commend and promote men because they are exceptional, how much more God, He would promote or put His people on display. He put Daniel on display in the palace of the king. It was of common knowledge that Daniel was a believer in Jehovah God. That is why the jealous governors could scheme, to promulgate a law on worship, that they knew would make him fall foul of the law. However, because of his faith in God he was not perturbed by the law and still went ahead to worship as always.

Press Pass Being Just Good To Be Excellent

Therefore we also, since we are surrounded by so great a cloud of witnesses, let us lay aside every weight, and the sin which so easily ensnares us, and let us run with endurance the race that is set before us, looking unto Jesus, the author and finisher of our faith, who for the joy that was set before Him endured the cross, despising the shame, and has sat down at the right hand of the throne of God. (Hebrews 12:1-2)

Jesus had such a successful life while on earth, even before the cross. He healed the sick, cast out demons, making a public show of Satan and His agents and did not have to die to prove that He was powerful. However, he submitted Himself to be killed so that through Him all who believe in Him would be saved. He also resurrected and this is where He is outstanding, why? Because most professed gurus, men of God, leaders, and messiahs would stop without going beyond this point. They do well to help people to alleviate their pain and meet their needs but none has ever gone to the extent of dying and resurrecting for humankind. Jesus pressed pass just being good to offer Himself as a sacrifice for humanity. It is for this reason we are told from the scripture above to take inspiration from him. Focus on this fact that to be outstanding you need to give more than others are willing and able to give.

The Bible says, "There is no greater love than this that a man should lay down his life for his friends". Jesus alone can do this. That is not all, Jesus taught us in the gospels that we can go that extra mile in our expression of godliness.

"If anyone wants to sue you and take away your tunic, let him have your cloak also. And whoever compels you to go one mile, go with him two" (Matthew 5:40 -41)

This is the practical application of the principle of excellence, He teaches, that when it comes to the virtues we espouse as His believers, there is not an end to them. In fact, this is applied in all the other components that form the life we live, be it in our marriages, businesses, churches, bringing up our children and so on. We cannot quit at anytime because we have had enough; it takes that extra mile to be outstanding. This principle is of the highest importance because it is in the preparation of the grounds, even before we start building. Asking of an extra mile would sometimes mean digging deep, but let us put it this way, if your life were a building, would it be the type everyone would wish to own? It is worth building with excellence, as this is evidence of the one to whom we belong.

Develop the passion to build

The reason God would show us in part what He has planned to do in our lives is to whet our appetite and begin to yearn for it and in turn, develop the passion to play our part to see it manifested. Denis Diderot puts it this way; "Only passions, great passions, can elevate the soul to great things." An individual's passion to get his or her life built to the architect's design comes when we understand, and in our mind's eye, can figure out what the outcome would be like. No one can develop a passion for you since it stems from a deep belief and conviction in what the outcome of a thing is going to be. From the days of the patriarchs until now, anytime God asks a person to do something, He will show him or her what to do. This may not be as He did to Moses, but by any means, we can capture, He does reveal it. It is either a strong desire or a dream that burns in our heart.

A Mental Picture Of The Desired Results Creates Passion

It did not come as a shock that after they had returned with a confirmation of what God had spoken about, they had a 'but' about it. Moreover, you will know the reason why from the verses below.

And they returned from spying out the land after forty days. Now they departed and came back to Moses and Aaron and all the congregation of the children of Israel in the Wilderness of Paran, at Kadesh; they brought back word to them and to all the congregation, and showed them the fruit of the land. Then they told him, and said: "We went to the land where you sent us. It truly flows with milk and honey, and this is its fruit. Nevertheless the people who dwell in the land are strong; the cities are fortified and very large; moreover we saw the descendants of Anak there. The Amalekites dwell in the land of the South; the Hittites, the Jebusites, and the Amorites dwell in the mountains; and the Canaanites dwell by the sea and along the banks of the Jordan."

Then Caleb quieted the people before Moses, and said, "Let us go up at once and take possession, for we are well able to overcome it."
But the men who had gone up with him said, "We are not able to go up against the people, for they are stronger than we." And they gave the children of Israel a bad report of the land which they had spied out, saying, "The land through which we have gone as spies is a land that devours its inhabitants, and all the people whom we saw in it are men of great stature. There we saw the giants (the descendants of Anak came from the giants); and we were like grasshoppers in our own sight, and so we were in their sight."
(Numbers 13:25-33)

They had a poverty-stricken mentality and as a result, chose to see what they considered negative over all positives. They saw the sons of Anak, the giants and perceived themselves as grasshoppers in their sight, and this confirms their pessimistic outlook on issues. The Israelites had not engaged them in battle yet so how did they assess their strengths against the enemy. It was in their thinking. They just perceived wrongly and that affected them later. They failed to use the opportunity to develop a passion to possess the land, thus they saw events differently.

The Anticipation of Results Produces Passion

You would not understand why Moses would send spies upon God's command, into the Promised Land, ahead of the rest of the multitude. Let us get acquainted with those verses of scripture:

Then Moses sent them to spy out the land of Canaan, and said to them, "Go up this way into the South, and go up to the mountains, and see what the land is like: whether the people who dwell in it are strong or weak, few or many; whether the land they dwell in is good or bad; whether the cities they inhabit are like camps or strongholds; whether the land is rich or poor; and whether there are forests there or not. Be of good courage. And bring some of the fruit of the land." Now the time was the season of the first ripe grapes. (Numbers 13:17-20)

The spies who Moses chose from each of the tribes of Israel were to have a fore taste of what was in store for the rest of the people. They were supposed to bring fruits and food from the land to convince the people that it was a far better land than where they were. The strategy God adopted, was to enable them develop the confidence to move into the land of promise, which at the same time was unknown to the people. God still uses this strategy today, He will most of the time give you a foretaste of what must happen, and in the case of building our lives, how our life is meant to turn out if we would follow Him step by step, precept upon precept, line upon a line. God knew based on an experience with the people of Israel that, just telling them to go into the land would prove difficult without evidence of what the land looked like. Therefore, He provided the evidence to convince them that the land really existed.

See Right To Develop Your Passion!

When God wanted Abraham to have an idea of the descendants, He was going to give him; this is what he did;

After these things the word of the LORD came to Abram in a vision, saying, "Do not be afraid, Abram. I am your shield, your exceedingly great reward." But Abram said, "Lord GOD, what will You give me, seeing I go childless, and the heir of my house is Eliezer of Damascus?" Then Abram said, "Look, You have given me no offspring; indeed one born in my house is my heir!" And behold, the word of the LORD came to him, saying, "This one shall not be your heir, but one who will come from your own body shall be your heir." Then He brought him outside and said, "Look now toward heaven, and count the stars if you are able to number them." And He said to him, "So shall your descendants be."(Genesis 15:1-5)

God gave Abraham a mental picture of what He had designed and planned. Abraham for the first time saw rightly. He saw beyond his own capabilities and intelligibility and saw through the eyes of God – by faith. Seeing right is seeing through the eyes of God. This experience was to develop in Abraham an excitement and a passion to cooperate with God to see the plan and design accomplished. Because developing a passion involves God giving you a glimpse of what the finished product would look like you need to see right – by faith.

I have asked myself a few times during my quiet moments why people like Apostle Peter would allow himself to be crucified upside down according to church history. There were believers who stood firm in their faith in Christ and were sawn asunder, others were deep-fried alive, and others were given to hungry lions to be fed upon and so on. It should be a passion for what they believe in. They saw a better life beyond the present through their faith in Christ.

Put Your Passion to Work

Take a more contemporary example in the life of Dr. Martin Luther King jr. in a speech he delivered on the 28th August 1963 at the Lincoln Memorial, Washington D.C. This speech is famously referred to as "I have a dream". There are portions that are of interest to what we have been discussing about passion. *"... Go back to Mississippi, go back* to Alabama, go back to South Carolina, go back to Georgia, go back to Louisiana, go back to slums and ghettos of our northern cities, knowing that somehow this situation can and will be changed.... I have a dream that my four little children will one day live in a nation where they will not be judged by the colour of their skin but by the content of their character. ... This is our hope, and this is the faith that I go back to the south with. With this faith, we will be able to hew out of the mountain of despair a stone of hope. With this faith, we will be able to transform the jangling discords of our nation into a beautiful symphony of brotherhood. With this faith, we will be able to work together, pray together, knowing that we will be free one day"*[5]*.

Dr. King's passion for freedom and enjoyment of the basic civil rights for the people of black descent in America can be deciphered from excerpts of his speech. Due to what he could envisage to be the long-term benefits of their struggle as civil rights activists, they pursued with the struggle. He was unlawfully jailed several times alongside many other ordinary black people. There is no question that this was passion at work. The results of their struggles were indeed the motivating element in their push for freedom, notwithstanding the fact that they could pay with their lives as others did during the struggle.

The more intriguing bit was the speech he delivered on April 3 1968, in Memphis a day before his assassination, he had this to say; *"Well I don't know what will happen now. We have some difficult days ahead. But it doesn't matter with me now because I have been to the mountaintop. And I don't mind. Like anybody, I would like to live a long life. Longetivity has its place. But I'm not concerned about that now I just want to do God's will. He's allowed me to go up to the mountain. And I've looked over. And I've seen the Promised Land. I may not get there with you. But I want you to know tonight, that we as a people will get to the Promised Land. And I'm happy tonight. I'm not worried about anything. I'm not fearing any man. Mine eyes have seen the glory of the coming of the Lord"[6].*

With this kind of speech, many agree he knew he would pay for freedom with his life, and yet he was defiant.

A person without passion often times does not have a reason to live. To build a life according to the architect's plan and design, you need passion as the examples above depict, passion that defies suffering and any form of obstacles. We need to encourage ourselves with the verses from Romans 8:18 *"For I consider that the sufferings of this present time are not worthy to be compared with the glory which shall be revealed in us."* Keep your eye on the prize.

Clear Up Your Space

casting down arguments and every high thing that exalts itself against the knowledge of God, bringing every thought into captivity to the obedience of Christ,

2 Corinthians 10:5

As part of physical land preparation before a structure is put up, the land on which the structure will be is cleared and leveled to make it easier to lay the foundation. Similarly, in preparing ourselves to build, we need to get rid of mentalities and habits that would sabotage our efforts to build a solid life. Clearing up your space in the contest of the core paradigm of this book, where the builder is also the building, has to do ridding our lives of anything that can stand in the way of the commencement of the building you envision to put up. This begins with the mind.

Everything Begins In The Mind

For as he thinks in his heart, so is he. (Proverbs 23:7)

This scripture above is quite self-explanatory. You are what you think, and you become what you think. The things you think about are things you have given audiences to in your mind, as thoughts cannot force themselves on a person. Therefore, the solution is to choose what you expose yourself to, either audiovisually or otherwise. We all have thoughts based on our exposure. To think about things that will help you build your life, is to choose to expose yourself to the kind of things that will assist you in that regard.

Beyond the thoughts that we think is the framework within which these thoughts occur and this is what we refer to as mentality. Mentality has to do with a way or mode of thought. The things we think about are equally important as the way we think about them. Therefore, a thought may not be necessarily be evil and yet the framework within which it is taken and the interpretations placed upon it makes it unproductive. Therefore, for instance, when we talk about poverty mentality, we are talking about a mode of thought that is not productive. Therefore, there is the need to develop the ability to penetrate your established mode of thinking and develop a new set of thinking that falls in line with the kind of building you intend to put up. Retain right thoughts and mentality to build a solid life, it is a choice; choose to develop that ability now.

Not only does the application of clearing up your space deal with the issues of the mind, it also has some spiritual inferences too. To do this, we would follow through some of the actual physical actions taken in the process of land clearing, namely: removing stumps, dislodging rocks, gathering and burning thorns, weeds and stumps and breaking up the ground to explain what our responsibilities are.

Processes

1: **Remove the stumps.**

Have you ever cut down a tree and prepared its trunk for construction or firewood? It is hard work. However, removing stumps is even harder. You must dig down and cut each of the main roots with an axe, machete, or chain saw. From a spiritual outlook, stumps are like elements or works of the flesh we have in our lives that cause us to stumble and fall. The stumps could also obstruct the foundation digging. Where the stumps are ignored, they may sprout again and grow into a tree on the site, although they may not be needed. What has been growing in your heart lately? Is it jealousy, envy, hatred, lust, greed, strife, adultery, heresies, outburst of wrath? These must be rooted out so that they do not endanger our lives and obstruct the building.

2: **Dislodge The Large Rocks**

There are times that in the preparation of a land for building, you come upon some large immovable rocks. If you seriously intend to build, it will require considerable digging and horsepower to move the rocks from the field. It may be very hard work, but it is worth it.

These rocks represent those elements in our lives that obscure our understanding of God's purpose for our lives or even threaten to prevent them from happening. This may include the associations and community, in which we find ourselves, habits, addictions and certain weaknesses in our lives.

You may find yourself in a company of people who because of one situation or the other have given up on their lives and are 'going nowhere'. Sometimes extreme poverty and many failed attempts to prominence and success by people in some communities make every one growing up in that community think it is impossible to make it big in any chosen field of endeavour. In this instance, you may have to choose to have mentors outside of your community who has attained what you want to attain. What you can see has a great influence on what you build. Therefore, make the effort to take out your life anything that obscure your view of God's plan and purpose for your life.

As you have ploughed your heart in the previous section, if you have discovered some large rocks that need to be removed, such as additions, habits and some personal weaknesses, seek help. You may want to talk to your pastor, a mature believer, or a professional about the problem. They may have some knowledge and experience of moving rocks such as these and be of immense help.

3: Gathering And Burning Thorns, Weeds And Stumps

There are times that land earmarked for building may lie fallow for so many years before the project commences. Therefore, it may be covered with thorns or other weeds and has to be removed and burnt even before the ground is broken. For this to happen a combination of approaches will have to be used depending on who is building.

In some advanced societies, these weeds and thorns are made into compost, which serves other agricultural purposes elsewhere.

The spiritual import of this is that these weeds, thorns represent those elements in our lives that are a constant reminder of our state before God. They are the things that annoy us by its pricking, telling us we have left some important issues in our lives unattended to. In as much as these remind us of our humanity and imminent weakness associated with it, we need to work hard to get rid of them from our lives to enable us to build our lives as it appears on God's plan for us.

4: Breaking Up The Ground

For a foundation to be laid the ground must be broken through digging either by a pickaxe or by a machine in the areas indicated on the plan of the architect. Without the breaking, it is impossible to lay the foundation. Since the clearing up of your space has to do with ourselves from the paradigm postulated by this book, breaking up the ground, refers to breaking the hardness of ones heart. Let us examine the scripture below.

For You do not desire sacrifice, or else I would give it;
You do not delight in burnt offering.
The sacrifices of God are a broken spirit,
A broken and a contrite heart—
These, O God, You will not despise.
(Psalm 51:16-17)

David wrote this scripture after God had confronted him for killing of Uriah - one of the general's in Israel's army to conceal an act of adultery with Bathsheba who was Uriah's wife. After being confronted by the Prophet Nathan about the issue, David breaks down in repentance and submission to God. God requires from us a broken and a contrite heart. Where is the hardness of your heart? If you have been hurt in a relationship or by your boss, father or mother, you may have sealed off an area of your life because it is just too painful. However, you need to let God break up those old resentments and heal those old hurts.

There are times we have been hardened by unbelief. You prayed that parent, child, grandparent or a friend would not die, and it happened, to the contrary. In addition, you may have concluded that God does not answer prayers, at least for you. Maybe you have been out of work because of the global financial crisis or have chronic illness that has taken its toll on your faith. The hardness of your heart must be faced squarely and broken up to allow the foundation to be laid and your building put up. Heartfelt repentance and confession are one way of digging deep. When is the last time you were literally on your knees broken before the Lord?

Your Mentality Is the Ceiling of Your Building

Continuing from where we left off about the mind, your mentality allows you to decipher information, which you act upon as an action, which consolidates into a lifestyle and lifestyle into destiny. There is no way you can build a new life, with an old mode of thought. As we saw in the previous subsection concerning Abraham, to alter his future, God asked him to come out of the tent. You will remain the way you are until you challenge yourself out of the mentality you have. Expose yourself to a new way of thinking and change your actions to change your life. You can only build a solid life with the right mentality. Clear up your life of all the clutters and get ready, to build according to the design of the supreme architect has shown to you. You will not be able to build a meaningful life without the right mentality for living. Think positively, think right and keep on thinking right because according to William James, "there is a law in psychology that if you form a picture in your mind of what you would like to be, and you keep and hold that picture there long enough, you will soon become exactly as you have been thinking". According to Brian Tracy, "the law of substitution says, your mind can hold only one thought at a time, positive or negative. You can substitute a positive thought for a negative thought whenever you choose".

Furthermore, he adds, "you can apply this law by deliberately thinking about something positive whenever you want to cancel out a thought or feeling that makes you angry or unhappy".[7]

Bear in mind that your mentality determines your altitude in life. In other words, how high you can go in life is determined by your mentality.

Do Not Remove the Ancient Landmarks

Do not remove the ancient landmark, which your fathers have set. (Proverbs 22:28)

The clearing up process should be done with great caution, as there are things that must remain to make the building process a success. We would consider some of these important virtues as landmarks. These include the virtues of the believer, which has been enumerated in Galatians 5:22-23. Though these verses do not contain all the virtues, they are pointers to what we can identify as landmarks when we come across them in scripture.

Landmarks Gives You the Perimeters of Your Freedom

These words of caution came at a time when it was easy for an individual to go to his piece of land and try to increase its dimensions by repositioning the landmark. You will have to understand that in ancient times they used stones and plants as landmarks. In recent times, concrete pillars are used in some places for demarcation. Landmarks are objects placed on a land to mark the boundary of a parcel of land. Landmarks are for two main purposes; first to show the extent or size of the land. With this, you know which portion does and does not belong to you. It tells you which area on the vast land you can and cannot work as it gives you the area of operation.

Landmarks Shows Who Owns You

In some regions of the world where concrete pillars are used as land marks. The initials of individuals who own the land on both sides are engraved on the pillar. Correspondingly, God has placed certain virtues and principles as landmarks in scripture that if we apply them would set the boundaries for our lives. It therefore suggests that there are parameters to the design and plan of God for our lives in the same way as the landmarks serve as boundaries. As we have already mentioned, the application and observation of those principles and virtues respectively in our lives would also reveal to whom we belong. We live in a time where people keep flip-flopping, as long as they get what they want, without conviction. This need not to be so, set your boundaries for all to see.

Bear Fruit That Identifies You to Your Source

There are nonetheless, principles God has set in His Word that show the way a person lives. The virtues visible in his or her life therefore bear an indication of where he or she belongs.

"Beware of false prophets, who come to you in sheep's clothing, but inwardly they are ravenous wolves. You will know them by their fruits. Do men gather grapes from thornbushes or figs from thistles? Even so, every good tree bears good fruit, but a bad tree bears bad fruit. A good tree cannot bear bad fruit, nor can a bad tree bear good fruit. Every tree that does not

bear good fruit is cut down and thrown into the fire. Therefore by their fruits you will know them. (Matthew 7:15-20)

One cannot profess to be something and yet his or her lifestyle points to something else. Nevertheless, the whole scripture in context is centred on one thing; the tree which is the source of the fruit. A Fruit is of the highest importance but its goodness or unwholesomeness is dependent on the tree it grew from. That is to say, that the source you belong or plug into will determine which virtues and lifestyle you demonstrate. Therefore, if you want to change the properties of the fruit you will need to change the properties of the tree. If you want a different fruit, you must go to the tree that can bear you that fruit. Since every particular tree would only bear a particular fruit.

Landmarks are Set, Fruits Are Born

The similarities of landmarks with the bearing of fruit, is that they both reveal the ownership and source respectively. There are two main sources of our outward behaviour or lifestyles; the flesh and the spirit as revealed in the Book of Galatians;

But if you bite and devour one another, beware lest you be consumed by one another!

I say then: Walk in the Spirit, and you shall not fulfil the lust of the flesh. For the flesh lusts against the Spirit, and the Spirit against the flesh; and these are contrary to one another, so that you do not do the things that you wish. But if you are led by the Spirit, you are not under the law. Now the works of the flesh are evident, which are: adultery, fornication, uncleanness, lewdness, idolatry, sorcery, hatred, contentions, jealousies, outbursts of wrath, selfish ambitions, dissensions, heresies, envy, murders, drunkenness, revelries, and the like; of which I tell you beforehand, just as I also told you in time past, that those who practice such things will not inherit the kingdom of God. But the fruit of the Spirit is love, joy, peace, longsuffering, kindness, goodness, faithfulness, gentleness, self-control. Against such there is no law. And those who are Christ's have crucified the flesh with its passions and desires. If we live in the Spirit, let us also walk in the Spirit. Let us not become conceited, provoking one another, envying one another. (Galatians 5:16-26)

You need to take note of certain words used in the verse 19 "works of the flesh" and verse 22 "fruit of the Spirit". The word works suggest an effort or energy being applied to produce that lifestyle. This speaks more of our natural human effort to live off our lives as humanly as possible. In other words, this is how good we can be. We cannot be any better than what our capabilities would allow.

On the other hand, the verse 22 "fruit of the Spirit" suggests that those virtues namely; love, joy, peace, longsuffering, kindness, goodness, faithfulness, gentleness and self-control come due to the workings of the Holy Spirit in us. These virtues, principally identify us with our source or to whom we belong. We must pay attention to these virtues presented in the verses of scripture above but more importantly endeavour to exhibit it all the time. We would agree with Xenophon (434BC – 355BC) who says, "If you consider what are called the virtues in mankind, you will find their growth is assisted by education and cultivation." We need to get involved to grow the fruits we bear by the Holy Spirit by remaining in Him and walking in obedience.

PART

T W O

Starting off with the Work

The reward of a thing well done is
to have done it.
RALPH WALDO EMERSON

2

Digging Up the Ground for the Foundation

If you have built castles in the air,
your work need not be lost; that is
where they should be. Now put the
foundations under them.

- Henry David Thoreau

Every Construction Have A Foundation

The life of a believer is in comparison to the construction of a building in many places in the Bible. If life is likened to a building then as in the physical construction of a building, the first and most important part of any permanent structure is its foundation. Unfortunately, most of us are constructing our lives without a foundation. In some cases what we refer to, as the foundation upon which we are building is no foundation at all.

The word foundation is defined "as a body or a ground upon which something is built up or overlaid". Another definition says, "It is a basis upon which something stands or is supported"[8].

As we may be aware of, foundations are of extreme importance because a foundation anchors your house to the earth, holding it down. Surprisingly, houses are likely to blow away in a windstorm and or are likely to sink into the ground where foundations have not been laid properly. Where ground water is high up the table, it has devastating consequences. But foundations do more than just hold a house, they must resist water, ice, fungus, insects and soil gases, and they have to stand up to soil pressures that can exert far more force than the weight of the house itself. It is for this reason that a geotechnical team is normally sent to assess an area as part of planning to determine the feasibility of constructing certain types of buildings in certain areas. These are all done to prevent defects from occurring in future resulting from foundation failures due to an outside force.

Have You Built Your Foundation Yet?

A builder cannot ignore this part of the construction process, if he or she intends to construct a long lasting, enduring, time tested building for posterity. Unfortunately, in many cases, this is not the case in our individual lives. The fact is either we are not aware of the direct application of foundations in our lives or do not even know what constitutes a foundation and how to cast it in our lives. According to the Builder's Foundation Handbook, "the foundation of a house is somewhat invisible and sometimes an ignored component of the building. It is increasingly evident; however, that attention to good foundation design and construction has significant benefits to the home owner and the builder, and can avoid some serious future problems"[9]. It adds, "Good foundation design and construction practice means not only insulating to save energy, but also providing effective structural design as well as moisture and termite control techniques where appropriate"[10].

Sometimes you can come across a building that has collapsed and beneath this mass of ruins; the reason for the failure lies buried, a bad foundation. It was unable to support the fine edifice, on the building plan, due to a foundation with defects. The same holds for foundations in our lives. Therefore, when we have laid a very good and strong foundation in our lives we have a very strong, stable and productive life. The question is 'what is that foundation and how can it be laid in our lives'.

Consider Laying "The foundation"

There are times when people say, "I'm building a good foundation for my life" and this may mean educating oneself, or investing in stocks or developing the right attitude. There are times we have thought that by educating our children or providing amenities for our local communities we are laying the foundation for socio-economic and even political development. However, does this action qualify as the foundation? As you may learn, all these are very good but are part of frames and not the foundation. It is part of the building upon the foundation. The scriptural text below provides a vivid answer to the foundation we require.

For no other foundation can anyone lay than that which is laid, which is Jesus Christ.
(1Corinthians 3: 11)

There is no other foundation apart from Christ. That which is supposed to serve as the foundation for everything in life has already been set up. In other words, nothing else can be considered as a foundation if it is not Jesus Christ. It does not matter how laudable, audacious and strategically astute it may be. It can form part of the building but not the foundation, because there is only one foundation.

In the context of the scripture, Paul was talking about having laid a foundation with the message of the cross[11] and that Jesus Christ was the foundation, the basis of salvation. This verse is also universally applied to every other thing that is built, in the sense that Christ is the foundation, not only of our salvation but also of our beings. If you want to lay a foundation for your children, introduce Christ into their lives, so it is with marriage, education and everything else we build in life. Being without Christ is like constructing a building without a foundation.

Lay 'The Foundation' For Your Life

To make Christ the foundation of your life, is to make Him the ground upon which every thing in your life is built. He becomes the central point in your life where everything else emanates and receives strength and support. You lay the foundation of Christ in your life by accepting Jesus Christ as your Lord and Personal Saviour. When the time of accepting Christ comes, people say, 'I want to stop sleeping around first, I want to stop stealing, smoking, drinking et cetera before He can come in, because He's holy and will not want the state I am in. The truth is that, no one invites a cleaner into his or her house after the house is clean; it is when the place is dirty and needs cleaning. You do not need to stop all you are doing wrong, before inviting Him into your life. When He comes in, He will clean you up beyond recognition. It is so simple but significantly spiritual, just a prayer away. The verse below carries that message.

"That if you confess with your mouth the Lord Jesus and believe in your heart that God has raised Him from the dead, you will be saved. For with the heart one believes unto righteousness, and with the mouth confession is made unto salvation". (Romans 10:9-10)

As you believe that, He is able to save you and confess this with your mouth, apart from receiving salvation for your soul, He becomes the foundation upon which your life is built, and a conscious effort must be made to remain in Him.

But you, beloved, building yourselves up on your most holy faith, praying in the Holy Spirit, 21 keep yourselves in the love of God, looking for the mercy of our Lord Jesus Christ unto eternal life. (Jude 20:21)

Jesus Christ is our surest faith upon whom we are built in addition to every other thing. Once again, it is clear from the book of Jude that Christ is the foundation and the foundation, which we must build upon. Moreover, this takes some action and activity from us. Of the many things, we said in the construction of buildings, measurements of dimensions and testing of soil gases. In our lives, we need not do any of these things because God in Jesus Christ already provides the foundation. The next stage is to abide upon that foundation through aligning our value systems to His value system.

Align Your Value Systems to The Value System Of The Kingdom Of God

When we have accepted Christ as the foundation for our lives, we need to abide in Him. We need to live our lives centred on Him. By this, we live off our lives reflecting his values in spirit and in letter. The result is that you become a new person and therefore like Him (Jesus). It is for this reason we accept that Christ is supra cultural. This means that the principles taught by God in Christ are applicable within every culture and makes persons better than they used to be. We would agree that, we develop sets of values that are a reflection, of how we evolve. These values are enforced by what our community and society accept as part of their domestic code for living in reasonable harmony with other members of our community and society. It is at this point that our community or society expects us to reflect those qualities of behaviour taught, and character that society regards as being intrinsically good, having desirable results, and worthy of emulation by others[12]. So we function primarily within a community and society that becomes the judge of our actions which are ultimately, influenced by our value systems. The question that arises is; what happens if the community or society's judgement is in error? It therefore suggests there will be no point of reference. There is no suggestion that cultural values must be scrapped; rather they can align with the value systems of God's kingdom to which we belong. This makes it imperative to make the values of God's Kingdom the point of reference since there is no error associated with it.

Begin the Process of Alignment

The process of alignment begins with an effort to change our way of thinking. Christ initiated this in His calls for repentance. The Greek word *metanoia* rendered as repent means 'a change of mind'. It is without doubt that we conceive our beliefs and with time, these consolidate into values. Therefore, if we can change what we believe we would change what we place value on, and ultimately exit the maze of struggles of modern living. Ronald Reagan puts it precisely this way that "The ultimate determinant in the struggle now going on for the world will not be bombs and rockets but a test of wills and ideas - a trial of spiritual resolve: the values we hold, the beliefs we cherish and the ideals to which we are dedicated."

Many people are continually suffering in our world because of injustice, neglect of their needs as orphans, voiceless because they are poor, marginalised because they are few because of the values people hold. If we can be dedicated to aligning our values to the values of God's kingdom, we would find peace and happiness in this world as God has intended it to be.

Apply The Law of Exchange

Jesus implicitly and explicitly teaches us so much about the aligning of one's value system to that of God's Kingdom from the verse below.

"Do not lay up for yourselves treasures on earth, where moth and rust destroy and where thieves break in and steal; but lay up for yourselves treasures in heaven, where neither moth nor rust destroys and where thieves do not break in and steal. For where your treasure is, there your heart will be also. (Matthew; 6:19-21)

A treasure is something of great worth or value. In this instance, a treasure could be anything on which we place value. This could include money, education, our bodies, our citizenship, time, strength, wisdom, gifts, talents and contacts and so on.

Jesus in His teaching is not against both the possessions and resources we have, because he implies neither of them to be evil nor of the issue that the possessions themselves are bad, but that a higher priority demands our resources. Jesus Christ was not teaching us to dismiss the importance of prosperity and ownership of material things. Your houses, happy family, highflying job, successful business and social status are not a threat to Him and the Kingdom of God.

You may be celebrated by men and yet be bankrupt with God. God is a Spirit and so how can we humans please Him let alone store up treasures in a place our physical eyes can never see? This is where the law of trade comes in, meaning that you exchange what is important to God with what you have.

Give What You Have For What God Has

If we take the instance of Cornelius in the Book of Acts of the Apostles, quoted below, his physical alms to poor people created a treasure in the spirit before God.

There was a certain man in Caesarea called Cornelius, a centurion of what was called the Italian Regiment, a devout man and one who feared God with all his household, who gave alms generously to the people, and prayed to God always. About the ninth hour of the day he saw clearly in a vision an angel of God coming in and saying to him, "Cornelius!"
And when he observed him, he was afraid, and said, "What is it, lord?" So he said to him, "Your prayers and your alms have

come up for a memorial before God. (Acts 10:1-4)

He had exchanged a physical possession with a spiritual treasure, which God says has become a memorial before Him. Whatever you possess, whether it is wisdom, strength, education, money, connections etc., you can use it to get eternal treasure, provided you can make that count in the sight of God. The aligning process is identifying the things God considers important and considering them important too.

This would only be possible by what God has revealed in His Word, the scriptures.

Cast Your Foundation By The Word Of God

God cannot be separated from His Word, because He is His Word, this evidence we gather from the gospels, one of which has been referred to below.

In the beginning was the Word, and the Word was with God, and the Word was God. He was in the beginning with God. All things were made through Him, and without Him nothing was made that were made.

And the Word became flesh and dwelt among us, and we beheld His glory, the glory as of the only begotten of the Father, full of grace and truth. (John 1:1-3, 14)

With this as the basis of our understanding of the role

of the word, Jesus makes a statement, which puts His word into perspective.

Therefore whoever hears these sayings of Mine, and does them, I will liken him to a wise man who built his house on the rock: and the rain descended, the floods came, and the winds blew and beat on that house; and it did not fall, for it was founded on the rock.

"But everyone who hears these sayings of Mine, and does not do them, will be like a foolish man who built his house on the sand: and the rain descended, the floods came, and the winds blew and beat on that house; and it fell. And great was its fall."

And so it was, when Jesus had ended these sayings, that the people were astonished at His teaching, for He taught them as one having authority, and not as the scribes. (Matthew 7:24-29)

In the scripture Jesus becomes the foundation upon which we build our lives through the word of God. We cannot say we are abiding upon the foundation if we are not living by the Word of God. The proof of our allegiance, loyalty and love for Christ Jesus who is also the foundation, is when we have wholly given ourselves to Him. The Word of God re-orients us through our beliefs and therefore helps us to develop new value systems. Through the Word, we can identify the things that are important to God and take them on as important so that while we lay up treasures in heaven, we are also establishing ourselves on the foundation in this life. All these happen in stages. It first begins by reading and studying God's Word or listening to God's Word and living by it, thus swapping your personal philosophies, ideologies and values in general with the principles of God's Word. This is a practical way of aligning our value systems to the value systems of God's Kingdom.

You Can Do It Too

Peter in Matthew 14 experiences the solidness of the Word of God as found below: "

And Peter answered Him and said, "Lord, if it is You, command me to come to You on the water." So He said, "Come." And when Peter had come down out of the boat, he walked on the water to go to Jesus. But when he saw that the wind was boisterous, he was afraid; and beginning to sink he cried out, saying, "Lord, save me!" And immediately Jesus stretched out His hand and caught him, and said to him, "O you of little faith, why did you doubt?" And when they got into the boat, the wind ceased. Then those who were in the boat came and worshiped Him, saying, "Truly You are the Son of God."

Peter's reliance on Christ's word was extraordinary, since he figured out that walking in Christ's command was safer and more stable than staying in the boat. He asks Jesus Christ to command him to come, meaning he was intending to walk on

His words.

Indeed, he stepped out of the boat, which was supposed to be relatively safer because it provided them some platform to hold onto. Peters' stepping out onto the sea was in response to Christ's command.

The lesson here is that we can hang unto God's word, even when our situation is as wobbly and unstable as Peters' in the boat on the sea. The Word of God becomes the solid foundation upon which we can build our lives and yet stand the test of times. The Word solidified under the feet of Peter because he obeyed the command.

Choose To Walk On Solid Ground

As you walk in obedience to God's Word, it will solidify under your feet, thus irrespective of the condition, which surrounds you; your foundation will be solid.

One thing from Jesus' teaching in Matthew 7:24-29 makes it clear that in this life, there are storms. The builders did not invite it nor did they expect it, but all the same, it came. The difference in the stories of the builders is their state of affairs after the rain, the wind and the storm. The wise builder's structure remained due to the foundation, the Word, which is also Christ as found in John 1:1-3.

From the beginning of the chapter, we related the foundation to building everything in our lives on it, including our marriage, families, personal finances, career, education and so on. This means, making the Word of God central in everything we do. The Word would take pre- eminence over what we feel, what we may even consider acceptable by our community and society. A renewing of our mind is essential and this can only be done by spending time in the Word of God and occupying our thoughts with His Word. By doing this, we are also programming our mind to think like our creator and to have an established framework for thinking and processing information, and subsequently, this would transcend into our actions.

3

Put up the Frame: Get the job done

The difference between a successful person and others is not a lack of strength, not a lack of knowledge, but rather a lack of will.
- Vince Lombardi

Inspiration does exist, but it must find you working.-
Pablo Picasso

Dreams never hurt anybody if you keep working right behind the dreams to make as much of them become real as you can. **- Frank W. Woolworth**

You Need Pillars

As you may know already, the life-building process is one that is done painstakingly and with some amount of uncertainty in the process. However, we know that the job would be finished with the help of the supreme architect – God, through Christ who is the author and finisher of our faith.

Every building should have pillars to sit on the foundation to prop the entire structure. A pillar restrains a structure from losing balance and eventually collapsing altogether. For a building to stand, it is imperative that at least three pillars are placed upon a well-prepared and planned foundation - if, it is to remain standing when pressure of any kind or from any direction is applied. In building, those who build upon a solid and secure foundation should on no account need to return to the foundational beginnings of the structure, if a problem in sturdiness arises. If structural issues in a building become ostensible over time, each pillar that is in place must first be looked at, and carefully inspected, as a probable source of a potential breech.[13] Once a good foundation has been established; moreover, today we have building codes to determine the uprightness of such - a permit is given. The building begins to be constructed, when the first pillar is placed, the second, the third and so on as required on the plan. The integrity of the final building or house - will be determined by the strength of the combined pillars, which then support the complete structure.

Know What Your Pillars Are

We would examine in this chapter those pillars you need to place in your life in relation to other people and pillars you need to place in your life solely for you. These would be discussed in no particular order because some intersect with others. In the scripture below, we find four unnamed men whose action attracted commendation from Jesus Christ. Their actions constitute some of the pillars we need in our building.

And again He entered Capernaum after some days, and it was heard that He was in the house. Immediately many gathered together, so that there was no longer room to receive them, not even near the door. And He preached the word to them. Then they came to Him, bringing a paralytic who was carried by four men. And when they could not come near Him because of the crowd, they uncovered the roof where He was. So when they had broken through, they let down the bed on which the paralytic was lying.
When Jesus saw their faith, He said to the paralytic, "Son, your sins are forgiven you."
And some of the scribes were sitting there and reasoning in their hearts, "Why does this Man speak blasphemies like this? Who can forgive sins but God alone?"

But immediately, when Jesus perceived in His spirit that they reasoned thus within themselves, He said to them, "Why do you reason about these things in your hearts? Which is easier, to say to the paralytic, 'Your sins are forgiven you,' or to say, 'Arise, take up your bed and walk'? But that you may know that the Son of Man has power on earth to forgive sins"—He said to the paralytic, "I say to you, arise, take up your bed, and go to your house." Immediately he arose, took up the bed, and went out in the presence of them all, so that all were amazed and glorified God, saying, "We never saw anything like this!" (Mark 2:1-12)

Jesus is the one we follow, He is our standard, therefore for us to impress Him like those men in the quoted text, and we need to be doing the same in principle not necessarily in letter as they did. Mark's gospel portrays Jesus not so much as the Messiah as others but as a model for all people[14]. He portrays Christ as someone who gave himself for people, spent time with them meeting their needs, teaching and empowering them. Although this text is not directly about the process of constructing a building, its import is significant for anyone who wants to build a life according to God's own design and approval. There are a few lessons we could learn from the four men in the text; they sacrificed for the comfort of another, they were anonymous, they knew how to handle the crowd, and they had a good sense of teamwork. It was this demonstration of their faith that attracted Jesus' commendation. We often talk the big talk, rhyme all the Christian jargons and yet get nothing done.

Thus, also faith by itself, if it does not have works, is dead. But someone will say, "You have faith, and I have works." Show me your faith without your works, and I will show you my faith by my works.(James 2:17-18)

Many people know what the plan of God is for their lives and yet are not doing anything about it. In putting up the frame to your life, these principles would help you remain strengthened until you finish. There is joy in living out the life God has ordained for you although it may involve some tedious but productive work.

Pillars

Pillar One: Sacrifice for the Comfort of Another

There is no evidence of these four men as relations to the paralysed man and besides, there were no fees charged for their efforts to ferry this man to Jesus. Certainly, they saw beyond the benefits they would personally get. After all what could be their gain? They were expending energy to carry a sick man to Christ for healing. For a reason under girded by the passion to help another, they decided they would be the ones through whom another person would experience the power of God or receive help. This is where many of us miss it; we will do things for people from whom we can get something back. These days some people feel its old fashioned to marry an individual with whom you can build a life together. Instead they look for 'an already made' man or woman to marry and do not care whether God approves it or not. Unsurprisingly, divorce rates are souring very high. In the United Kingdom, "one in five men and women divorcing in 2006 had a previous marriage ending in divorce. This proportion has doubled from what it used to be in 1981; just over one in ten men and women divorcing had a previous marriage ending in divorce. For all divorces granted, behaviour was the most common fact proven"[15].

I am not therefore suggesting that this is mainly the reason for divorce; however, it is a contributing factor. People will do anything to attract a rich man or woman to live the high life. It is also for this reason that pre-nuptial agreements are becoming popular. Rachel Lewis in the Daily Mail Newspaper confirms this, "high profile divorces ... have meant that some men are panicking at the thought of settlement. Hence, the rise in popularity of prenups – we have seen a 15 percent increase in our firm in the past year (2007). They are most popular with Celebes, wealthy businesspersons, lawyers, accountants, bankers and brokers. Agreements are especially common in second marriages where adult children suggest a prenups to protect their inheritance from their new step parent"[16]. As controversial as this subject may be in some quarters, the final conclusion is that those who go into marriage with the intention to make the life of the other better tend to succeed and not those with the intention to receive or take away seems to fail.

You are Someone's Miracle

Submitting yourself to the comfort of another is a real virtue and attracts the commendation of our Lord Jesus Christ. Just to let you know that miracles are made in heaven, but it is distributed by men. In other words, God uses us to meet the needs of people both in and beyond our immediate surroundings. Therefore, if we position ourselves well, then our hearts, mind, homes, bank accounts, businesses, churches, families could be that point of distribution. Bear in mind that you are not what you are for yourself. The anointing, wisdom, wealth, talents and even your children are for the benefit of others and the entire world. This is so that others would be blessed through you. The scripture has it in Matthew 5:16; "Let your light so shine before men, that they may see your good works and glorify your Father in heaven." This is so that men may see your good works and not so you can see your way, because the light is meant to shine for others. It is for others too apart from us that God sends good things our way.

The Attitude of Most Imminent Inventors: People First

Come to think about this; what if Thomas Edison had kept the invention of the light bulb to himself?

That is not all; today many lives are saved in hospitals around the world due to the availability of blood at blood banks. "The idea of a blood bank was pioneered by Dr. Charles Richard Drew (1904 – 1950). Dr. Drew was an American medical doctor and surgeon who started the idea of a blood bank and a system for the long-term preservation of blood plasma (found that plasma kept longer than whole blood). His ideas revolutionalised the medical profession and saved many lives. Dr. Drew set up and operated the blood plasma bank at the Presbyterian Hospital in New York City, NY. Drew's project was the model for the Red Cross system of blood banks, of which he became the first director"[17]. Stop thinking about yourself now and start searching for ways you can help someone if not the whole world. It is within your reach if only you can change your thinking.

You Can Make a Difference Too

Let us finally look at another inventor whose invention was of such a world-changing propensity. Benjamin Franklin (January 17, 1706 – April 17 1790) was an American statesman, writer, printer and inventor. Franklin experimented extensively with electricity. In 1752, his experiments with a kite in a thunderstorm led to the development of the lightening rod. Franklin started the first circulating library in the colonies in 1731. He also invented bifocal glasses and the Franklin stove. Benjamin Franklin first proposed the idea of daylight savings time in 1784"[18].

Like the men whose inventions are described above, you are an answer to someone's prayer for a miracle. Your life itself is a miracle. That individual who is not born again, who is searching for the real meaning of life is depending on you to get closer to him or her. That pregnant teenager who cannot cope with the pressure of being a teen mum is waiting for you to step into her life. The beggar in the street corner, that alcoholic you meet every night from church, the man or woman with that broken heart who needs comfort and encouragement. Reach out to someone today and relieve them of their pain. Step out and give out what you have. You are not here to add to the numbers to bring the world's population to 8 billion. Without you, the world is incomplete. Like a giant missing jigsaw puzzle, step up to the board and take your place. Is your next project, research, house you are going to buy, the business you are establishing, going to bless someone? Let wisdom lead you to find someone to help.

Follow This Example

The Apostle Paul gives us a perfect example of self-sacrifice. Jesus entered our history and our skins, to not only identify with us but to be our Saviour and Lord, our forgiver, redeemer and leader. It is with this in mind that Paul writes to encourage us to emulate Christ.

Therefore if there is any consolation in Christ, if any comfort of love, if any fellowship of the Spirit, if any affection and mercy, fulfill my joy by being like-minded, having the same love, being of one accord, of one mind. Let nothing be done through selfish ambition or conceit, but in lowliness of mind let each esteem others better than himself. Let each of you look out not only for his own interests, but also for the interests of others.

Let this mind be in you which was also in Christ Jesus, who, being in the form of God, did not consider it robbery to be equal with God, but made Himself of no reputation, taking the form of a bondservant, and coming in the likeness of men. And being found in appearance as a man, He humbled Himself and became obedient to the point of death, even the death of the cross.
(Philippians 2:1-5)

Your Sacrifice Magnifies Your Life

You may look very insignificant in size but your act of sacrifice would make you look big in the eyes of those who receive help from you. Jesus came from Nazareth an unimportant village and yet because of His sacrifice for humanity He has become an icon.

There are plethoras of ways we can emulate Christ. "In a riot that occurred in the La Mesa Prison in Tijuana, Mexico, thousands of inmates battled the guards with bottles and rocks, while the guard shot back with machine guns until a small American woman in her 70's walked into the middle of the war, raised her hands, and signalled for quiet. Remarkably, calm fell on the prison. That woman was Mary Brenner, who was raised in Beverly Hills. There she lived what she called a 'glamorous life' until she found Christ and followed Him in a completely new direction. Now she is known as Sister Antonia. She is a nun and lives in a sparse 10-foot cell inside the prison. She moved there 25 years ago to live among murders, thieves, and drug dealers. Sister Antonia has poured out her life for these prisoners, nursing their wounds, getting them eyeglasses and medicine, caring for their families, and washing their bodies for burial"[19].

She describes the experience simply as living out her calling. In an interview, she would say 'I wouldn't trade this cell for any place in the world'. If we as believers would have our hearts surrendered to God through lives of self-sacrifice, our churches would be healthy biblical communities that are overflowing with people flocking to be part of these self-sacrificing communities of God. Let us move on to the next pillar.

Pillar Two: Try to Be Anonymous

In our world today, we have misplaced priorities. There are times that one thinks most of the people we refer to as celebrities do not deserve to be so called. However, many people helping humanity in some of the remote places on this planet are hidden from the cameras of giant TV stations. These people may never appear on our TV screens of our day. Such was the attitude of these four men who carried the paralysed man to Jesus Christ. Not even their names are mentioned. Probably, the writer did not know their names or perhaps they had left the scene after the miracle, and could not be traced. They had accomplished their task end of story. Richard Morrison writes that "....... However, on Monday, the front page of The Times (and most other papers) was the reverse of that a huge montage of Britain's Olympic (2008) winners dominates radiating a feel good glow of success, exhilaration and pride. You hardly noticed the story at the foot of the page: a forecast that 300,000 British workers will lose their jobs as the recession bites. Furthermore, you could easily have missed the tiny paragraph tucked down the side of our pictured Olympic heroes. It told us, almost with an apologetic cough, that some 14 million people are starving to death in Africa, that made me think. Faced with an African famine, or thousands of casualties from yet another nasty turf-war between nationalistic thug-regimes, the temptation is to feel utterly helpless. Such horrors seem unpreventable. But luckily, many millions of people around the world do not give up in despair. In their small way, they show kindness to people. They collect for famine relief and give time to good causes. They campaign for justice. They show compassion to strangers. They try to infuse a sense of morality into children. They attempt to keep the politics of their own land honest and descent. Most of them will never win a medal. Yet they are far more imbued with the true Olympic spirit than the athletes out for personal glory in Beijing"[20].

Do Not Seek the Praise of Men

In true fashion, these four anonymous men in scripture like the scenario painted by Morrison, didn't go about announcing to everyone what they were doing, what introduced them were their actions. They knew who was supposed to be the centre of attention, the sick man. As you read now you may be working in a firm or belong to a church or group and be the one who makes all the difference behind the scenes, yet not seem to be recognised. Anna a widow mentioned in scripture (see text below) that, had been waiting on the Lord in the temple and making intercession for many years before ever being heard of. If it were not for the fact that, Jesus was brought to be dedicated, no one would have ever heard of her great work.

Now there was one, Anna, a prophetess, the daughter of Phanuel, of the tribe of Asher. She was of a great age, and had lived with a husband seven years from her virginity; and this woman was a widow of about eighty-four years, who did not depart from the temple, but served God with fastings and prayers night and day. And coming in that instant she gave thanks to the Lord, and spoke of Him to all those who looked for redemption in Jerusalem.(Luke 2:36-38)

Do not give up because men have not as yet recognised your work if God recognises it that should be enough. Because it is from Him that, all blessings flow. Set your eyes on the prize of your high calling and do not be distracted by those who want the praise of men.

Recognition Comes From Men But Promotion Comes From Above

Like David who killed a bear and a lion, no one knew about it. When the time for promotion came, he was chosen and promoted. He was sent from the backside of the desert to be anointed king. A quiet lifestyle is full of power since its not easy for people to figure out what your next move is going to be. The truth is that not all of us have our work acclaimed worldwide. The lack of this understanding would leave you disillusioned. If you can help someone without seeking recognition, you are on your way to affect lives in such a profound way. It is the craving for recognition, the need to enrich CV's et cetera that is why people are wary of whom they receive help. It seems people are always searching for ways to get to the top on the back of others. As a result, people no longer trust each other enough to ask for help when they need it. This has given rise to the setting up of anonymous rehabilitation centres, anonymous lawyers, anonymous doctors, anonymous this and anonymous that, to gain credibility with people. We can all restore trust in each other to go out of our way and help people. Would we be like the four anonymous men whom Jesus commended? We can emulate them with the help of Christ.

Pillar Three: Know How to Handle Your 'Crowd'

As these men set off with the paralysed man on the stretcher, their objective was to get to Jesus for the sick man to receive his healing. When they got to the entrance where Jesus was, they could not get in due to the crowd. There were people there who would not simply give them access for one reason or the other. Maybe granting them access meant being pushed to the back themselves, and this is why they would not. It was also possible that those in there were also searching for a miracle themselves.

As we build our lives, there are situations and things that seek to crowd us out of the plan of the supreme architect of our lives. They could see their miracle, goals and vision, but simply cannot get to it. The crowd is anything that hinders you from getting to that miracle you are seeking, the vision you want to accomplish, dreams you want to realise and the life you want to build. It comprises of even the most little things to the enormous things that prevent us from reaching our goals in life building. It seems like a paradox to say that the crowd represent small things.

Crowd

1. Do Not Ignore the Small Things And The Minor Details

Napoleon Hill author of 'Think and Grow Rich' said, "Before we can master an enemy, we must know its name, its habits, and its place of abode"[21]. He was simply talking about identifying the things that can become obstacles to our success no matter how big or small they are. We as human beings are prone to sometimes take care of the big things while we neglect other things, though little but of similarly big effect; the little foxes that destroy the vine (see Songs of Solomon 2:15).

According to an article written by Gladys Edmunds a columnist with the USA today, "we carry many habits, feelings and attitudes within, that can play a role in our success or failure. Let us take a look at one not often mentioned; dealing with minor details. Too often, the minor details are left to chance or forgotten completely. Furthermore, yet if you take care of the minor details all else can fall into place more easily"[22]. To overcome this situation, we need to do a self-evaluation often to be sure we have not left out anything negligible to the eye and yet could be the source of a total breakdown of the life we are building. The importance of this principle is true in biblical times with cities that the people of God spared; nations who were very small at the time but consequently grew to become big, out of which produced a champion in the person of Goliath who terrorised them for a long time.

2. Watch! The People You Cannot Stand

We all have our difficult people maybe at present or sometime in the past and may admit success or failure with the way we handled them. I do not claim to be an expert on this because I have blown it a few times myself, but what stands out of the lessons learnt is that people choose from a variety of behaviours that are dependent on the prevailing situation, just as they choose clothing for specific functions. Mostly a difficult person is someone who relates or works from the wrong side of their personality, rather than a conscious desire to be difficult. Although the latter may be true about some who due to their own personality disorder divert attention and focus to themselves through proving difficult. There are some who do that in order to settle a score, which may be unknown by the person, they hold the grudge against.

As we will later find out, teamwork is vital in any building process and therefore making an effort to understand people from their point of view is vital. When we change our attitude and behaviour of what we consider 'the odd ones', "we can find enough reason to improve in our ability to work effectively with people"[23], who we may have considered difficult.

Having said that, one of the ways that you can identify a difficult person, is their dogged determination to do things their way. In this instance no matter what anyone says or does, it does not matter; they will force their ideas on everyone else. Let us consider a few tips for dealing with negative aspects in others.

This Is How You Do It

When you see someone go into attack modes or excess defensiveness, recognise that it is useless to argue with him or her.

Realise that the person is feeling very insecure at that time.

Do not continue to push them because they will only get worse.

If the symptoms only seem to occur when the person is under stress, wait until another time to pursue the discussion.

If they are always overly defensive or always attacking others, you may need to find another person to work with who does not have the same problem. Keep your own sense of self-confidence and do not allow yourself to be verbally abused.

If the difficult person is your boss, reconsider whether its time to find a job elsewhere.

These tips would guide you, as you stand out of the crowd and move closer to attaining goals of productivity and fruitfulness.

3. Check your Belief Systems

What we believe can become the springboard to attain higher heights as well as the crowd against the attaining of our goals and building the life we want. A belief is defined as a "conviction of the truth of a proposition without its verification derived from perceptions, contemplations (reasoning) and communication"[24]. To have a better understanding of this definition we will again look at a few key words within this context; perception contemplations and communication.

Perception or worldview refers to the framework through which an individual interprets the world and interacts with it. Contemplations refer to reasoning and thinking. Communication refers to the interaction with the outside world.

In our attempt to breakdown the definition of belief system, we need to look further at the definition of system; "An entity maintains its existence and functions as a whole through the interaction of its parts"[25]. Therefore, the behaviour of a system depends on how the parts are related. This means that the way a system behaves is due to how each constituent part function. For example, the bed you sleep on whether it is made of wood, aluminium or steel, is made up with different parts. Because the constituent parts of the bed were shaped and cut in a way, that when put together makes the bed. Therefore, we can say that the parts make them what they are. Therefore, the belief system you have is a collective result of the way you view the world through your thinking processes due to your interaction with the world. If you have inferiority complex for instance, or you are lazy or fearful it is as result of your belief system. For you to change your actions and behaviour you need to change what you believe. In addition, this must be done because we are not born with belief systems we learn or imbibe it. Then and again as you make these changes to your thinking, there will be a change in behaviour. As Proverbs 23:7, "....as a man thinks so is he...."

Believe In Something Anyway

In his psychology of beliefs, David J. Schneider postulates that, "we recognise that a few beliefs that seem bizarre at one time become perfectly normal later. Most of our beliefs are essentially unproblematic in the sense that we do not question them or worry much about their validity. In fact, huge numbers of our beliefs seem so grounded in reality or so much a part of our culture that it seems silly to question them and an empty academic exercise to seek their sources. Furthermore, people hold anomalous beliefs with as much conviction as we hold our unproblematic beliefs, and they often turn the tables on us by suggesting that we are the people who are of touch with reality.[26].

Maintain your beliefs if it is productive but be ready to change when necessary, as this would set you up for success. As John Stuart Mill puts it, **"**One person with a belief is equal to a force of 99 who have only interests".

4. Avoid Sin: Missing the Target

The four men had a target in mind, and it was to get their sick man to Jesus. When they got to the entrance of the house, the crowd will not allow them to enter for one reason or the other. Consequently, at that point they could not reach their target. Moreover, this is where we could apply the fact that a crowd in a person's life can be sin. The biblical Greek word *hamartia* rendered in English as sin "is the most frequently used word for sin, occurring in its various forms about 227 times. When the writer wanted one inclusive word for sin, he used this one. The metaphor behind the word is 'missing the mark'[27]. Sin disconnects us from God; it keeps us away from the source of life itself.

And the LORD God commanded the man, saying, "Of every tree of the garden you may freely eat; but of the tree of the knowledge of good and evil you shall not eat, for in the day that you eat of it you shall surely die." *(Genesis 2:16-17)*

The expression 'die' did not only refer to physical death but an eternal separation from God. Therefore, we see that sin positions us away from God and therefore by application of the story of the paralysed man and the four men who carried him, sin closes the door or shuts our access to the source of life and livelihood. It is for this reason that the bible teaches us in Mark 11:25-26 "And whenever you stand praying, if you have anything against anyone, forgive him, that your Father in heaven may also forgive you your trespasses. However, if you do not forgive, neither will your Father in heaven forgive your trespasses." We need to be free of sin in order to be able to stand before God and be confident that He hears us when we pray. He is holy and nothing unholy can enter His presence.

Pursue peace with all people, and holiness, without which no one will see the Lord: (Hebrews 12:14)

Our state of holiness will be restored to our place of originality with God. By extending this application to other areas of our lives, sin could mean anything that prevents us from reaching God's standard of life for us. Therefore, it is a sin not to build the life God intends for you to build and fulfil the dream and vision we believe God has given to us.

There is clearly an issue of the original sin. It takes Jesus Christ to set a person free from sin, and this is by accepting him as Lord and personal Saviour of your life. What is interesting is that, when the word sin is used in the "Gospels it almost occurs in a context that speaks of forgiveness or salvation (see Matthew1:21; John1:29). When they finally got through to Jesus, He said 'son your sins are forgiven you'. It is important to note that we need to ask for forgiveness anytime we sin to bring about our restoration to our place in God.

Identify Your Crowd

To conclude this subsection on the crowd, we need to remind ourselves that the crowd could mean many different things to different people. This could include social, political, economic, and even cultural systems that hinder us from building the life God has ordained for us. The list could go on without an end. The truth is that, there are situations, circumstances and things that can crowd us out of our targets, solutions and answers we seek in life. In putting up the frame as part of the life building process, we will face the crowd, but it is at that moment that we look for alternatives and options to reach our targets or move to the next stage.

Pillar Four: Be Willing to Work Together With Others

As already established from the scripture, it is not clear what the relationship of these four men were. Whatever it was, they were willing to work together to achieve a goal. In the life-building process, people are essential because you may not possess all you need to accomplish your goal. You will need to fall on other people to help you. Let us analyse the scripture once again contextually and relate it to this principle under discussion; the paralytic was the substance of their assignment or the job that needed to be carried out. He was the problem they needed a solution to.

Their desired results would be a healed, strong man. The process to make this happen is that the paralysed man who cannot walk must get to the source of healing so the desired results can be realised and this is where the significance of the four men is identified. There had to be people who were willing to come together to make it happen.

Greatness Is Measured In How Much You Care About Humanity

For whatever vision you have or assignment you are engaged in you need others and their supplies to assist you to accomplish it. Whether it is a life, a church, business, family or leadership you are engaged in, you need others. Some of us run away from people because we fear problems. We sometimes think we have enough problems of our own to take on that of others. You need to understand as a matter of principle that others' problems may be your opportunity for prominence or elevation in life. Dr Drew would just be an ordinary man, dead and forgotten if not for solving humans' problem of storing blood for emergency use in future. It may not be possible to count the number of medical doctors the world has produced in the last century; there are only a few who stands out to be remembered among whom is Dr. Drew.

However, for these four anonymous men, this paralytic may not have received his healing ever and the four men would never have met Jesus on that personal level to receive commendation. We all need others to play their role to get things accomplished in our lives, and building our lives is not an exception to the application of this principle. Jesus taught this principle and lived by this principle, as He gave himself for humanity. Let us examine the scripture below:

Yet it shall not be so among you; but whoever desires to become great among you, let him be your servant. And whoever desires to be first among you, let him be your slave— just as the Son of Man did not come to be served, but to serve, and to give His life a ransom for many." (Matthew 20:26 -28)

Jesus laid down the principle for determining greatness; it is to serve and not to be served. It is being of use to humanity. I want to ask you a question to be answered irrespective of your age, social status, education and maybe public recognition. What have you contributed so far to humanity either alone or together with others? Look for something to do to help someone either on your own or with others.

Do You Have A Team For Your Building Project?

Richard Daft describes a team as "a unit of two or more people who interact and coordinate their work to accomplish a specific goal"[28]. In this sense, these men were a team with respect to the numerical composition. Further to this, there are few characteristics Draft's sets out, which serve as indicators of a team.

Indicator One: You Need Other Persons

In the business environment, the creation of synergies is a vital responsibility for managers. Good teams produce synergies that enhance the levels of productivity and to a large extent profitability. God recognizes a person or an individual who exhibits their openness to learn from others and for others to learn from them in order to get greater results. Whatever

God has called us to do we need one another. God may have given you a vision or assignment, you may assume the responsibility of leadership but a leader is not a leader without followers. The followers assist the leader to translate that, which exists, in his or her mind or on paper into reality. Therefore, there is the need to display mutual respect.

This next statement is going to make sense to you if you have ever been to a forest or seen one on TV etc. In a forest, there are big trees and often undergrowth comprising of different species and type of plants. Some of them are so tiny at the stems and their linear structure gives them no chance at all of experiencing direct sunshine. They coil around some of these big trees as they grow to reach to the very top. The lesson here to buttress the point made is that sometimes it takes another's ability, contacts, and gifts to get you to accomplish some things in life.

Indicator Two: You Must Get Involved With Others

Although there are no written records of the four men in our foundational scripture from Mark 2:1-5, communicating with each other, it might have surely happened. As we read from the verses, when the crowd prevented them from entering, they quickly climbed to the top of the building and then lowered the paralysed man down right in front of Jesus Christ.

In a group, church, business, family where there is regular interaction, there are many things accomplished because through interaction, we know what is on each other's mind and can agree or disagree. In the early church, one of their key practices was fellow- shipping together. Additionally, beyond meeting together they cared for each other, supported each other and bore one another up. This is the same for us, people want to be cared for, but do not want to be responsible for anyone or anything. In my experience as a pastor, those members who complain, no one calls them, they do not call or visit anyone.

Remember we need one another to get things accomplished. In building up our lives as in constructing a building, there are times different contractors with different areas of expertise to fix this or fix that have to be brought on board to execute the project. The principal contractors know they cannot do everything by themselves. In modern business, firms and organisations outsource at some stage of their production or even in marketing their products, to be sure of a high quality product or may even cut down on the total cost of production. What do you look out for when teaming up with others?

Indicator Three: You Must Have a Common Ground

The people who may come in at a point or stage in our life-building process are only coming to play their role and not to take over. It is when they have made their contribution that the goal would be reached. It does not matter how small their contribution is in your eyes, they get fulfilment because their own goal or God-ordained life is to supply what they have or possess, for the completion of a process of building someone's life. There are times people are wary of others coming into their lives to contribute because they fear these people will claim the glory and honour of the accomplishment. For a team to be effective - as already established in the analysis at the beginning of this section (pillar four) - there is the need to have a clear-cut goal. This way you will be able to identify what you need for the total accomplishment of your goal. To be successful at this stage we also need to acknowledge the people who are contributing, and what they are contributing, and make this known to them. Jesus response to the four men was phenomenal because this was not part of their agenda. It was to get the paralytic healed. Jesus took all these issues discussed into consideration before issuing the commendation to them. In the end, the output of their efforts was forgiveness and a sick body strengthened again. What shall be the result if you team up with the right people?

You Will Be Fulfilled By Accomplishing Things with Others

The four men were also pleased and satisfied that at least their efforts have been appreciated with a commendation from Jesus for a good work done. Indeed to move away from the crowd and climb unto the roof of the building with a sick man and even lower this man takes determination, effort and faith in the sense that they knew that if only they could get to Jesus the sick man would be healed. The crowd might have thought they were returning home probably because they did not see them on the grounds anymore. Rather, they were busy on the other side of the house where the crowd was much less looking for a way to the roof of the building. They succeeded eventually and were able to lower the sick man through the roof to Jesus, in the room where He was. You can kiss your crowd goodbye. You can show them how smart you are. You can open your eyes now to the minor details; learn to accommodate the people you cannot stand, change some belief systems you hold and turn away from sin. No doubt when you build these pillars, they would help you to put up a solid frame. In the end, and get the job done.

Pillar Five: Develop Self Discipline

From the foundational scripture of this book as quoted again below, there are a few inferences from which pillar five is derived.

For which of you, intending to build a tower, does not sit down first and count the cost, whether he has enough to finish it—lest, after he has laid the foundation, and is not able to finish, all who see it begin to mock him, saying, 'This man began to build and was not able to finish'? (Luke 14:28 – 30)

Jesus was teaching that building a tower has a cost to it and anyone who builds must first assess and analyse, not only the magnitude of the job (*sit down first and count the cost*) to be done, but also whether (*he or she has enough to finish it*) they personally have what it takes to finish. In most cases people who start out projects and do not finish lack self-discipline, in contrast to those who have accomplishments.

Understand What Self-discipline Is?

Self-discipline is "Training and control of oneself and one's conduct, usually for personal improvement".[29]

Indeed, in a tertiary school setting for instance, self-discipline is what distinguishes good students from bad ones. This shows in the quality of time spent on researching for their assignment and even studying for examinations. When we were in school, I remember during 'prep' time (a mandatory evening time of study usually for duration of three hours for all students in a boarding school) you always find this classmate of mine who cannot simply sit down behind his book for a period. He keeps roaming about making noise and distracting others and soon he was failing his assignments and examinations until he developed the discipline to sit and study.

Further, self-discipline in a person's life can be identified in many forms; which include his or her ability to keep focus in the face of distractions. There are two main areas to look at in developing self-discipline, namely Being Realistic and Having Will Power.

Being Realistic

Being realistic means that you perceive reality precisely and deliberately accept what you apprehend. The most basic mistake people make with respect to self-discipline is a failure to accurately perceive and accept their present situation. If you are going to succeed at weight training, for instance, the first step is to figure out what weights you can already lift. How strong are you right now? Until you figure out where you stand right now, you cannot adopt a realistic training program. If you have not deliberately accepted where you stand right now in terms of your level of self-discipline, it is highly improbable that you are going to ameliorate at all in this area.

Visualize a would-be bodybuilder who has no thought how much weight he or she can lift and arbitrarily adopts a training routine. It is in effect certain that the chosen weights will be either too weighty or too light. If the weights are too heavy, the trainee will not be able to lift them at all and thus will experience no muscle growth. On the other hand, if the weights are too light, the trainee will lift them easily but will not build any muscle in doing so.

Similarly, if you want to increase your self-discipline, you must know where you stand right now. How strong is your discipline at this moment? Which challenges are easy for you, and which are practically unattainable for you? Without being realistic, you get either ignorance or denial. With ignorance you simply do not know how disciplined you are — you have probably never even thought about it. You will only have a hazy notion of what you can and cannot do. You will experience some easy triumphs and some drab failures, but you are more likely to blame the task or blame yourself instead of simply acknowledging that the "weight" was too heavy for you, and that you need to become stronger.

When you are in a state of denial about your level of discipline, you are fastened into a deceitful view of reality. You are either overly negative or positive about your potentials. In addition, like the trainee who does not know his or her own strength, you will not get much better because it is unlikely you will be able to hit the correct training area by accident. On the negative side, you will only pick up easy weights and avoid the heavy ones which you could actually lift and which would make you stronger. Moreover, on the optimistic side, you will keep trying to lift weights that are too heavy for you and failing, and afterwards you may either beat yourself up or make up your mind to try harder, neither of which will make you stronger.

Have Willpower

Willpower is the expression of a convergent force to breakthrough an obstacle. You group up all your energy and make an immense push ahead. You strike your difficulties strategically at their weakest points until they crack, allowing you enough room to manoeuvre deeper into their territory and finish them off. Will power is much like any part of your physical body. If you use it consistently, and flex it, it will grow in size and strength, and even surprise you. If you do not use it, it will atrophy, wither, and disappear. When exercising as in the analogy used in the section of the self-discipline, no one grabs the heaviest weights first, when they are just starting out, people do not run an endurance contest the same day they buy their first pair of running shoes. With will power, start out small. Set goals, and challenge yourself—first in small things, then in large things. As you continue to flex the muscle of your will power, you will be startled at how easy self-discipline can become.

Over time, as with any habit, exercising your will power will become second nature. You will do it without even thinking about it, or planning it before hand. At that point, you will be a much more effective leader, decisive, bold, and enduring. You will no longer be distracted from your goals by bad habits or patterns of behaviour, because you will simply stamp them out with the iron force of your will.[30]

Practical Steps For Developing Your Willpower

Suppose your goal is to lose 35 pounds. You endeavour to go on a diet. It takes willpower, and you do okay with it the first week. However, within a few weeks you have fallen back into old habits and gained all the weight back. You try again with different diets, but the result is still the same. You cannot sustain momentum for long enough to reach your goal weight. That has to be expected though because willpower is transitory. It is for sprints, not endurance contests. Willpower requires conscious focus, and conscious focus is very draining — it cannot be maintained for long. You will eventually be sidetracked.

Here is how to tackle that same goal with the proper application of willpower.

Step One: You accept that you can only apply a short explosion of willpower maybe a few days at best. After that, it is gone. Therefore, you had better use that willpower to alter the territory around you in such a way that maintaining momentum will not be as hard as building it in the first place. You need to use your willpower to establish a foothold on the eighteen-yard box of the goal post before shooting for goal. Therefore, you sit down and make a plan. This does not require much energy, and you can spread the work out over many days.

Step Two: You single out all the various targets you will need to strike if you want to have a chance of success. First, all the junk food needs to leave your kitchen, including anything you have a tendency to binge on and you need to replace it with foods that will help you lose weight, like fruits and veggies.

Step Three: Secondly, you know you will be enticed to get fast food if you come home starving and do not have anything ready to eat, so you choose to pre-cook a week's worth of food in advance each weekend. That way you always have something in the refrigerator. You set aside a block of several hours each weekend to buy groceries and cook all your food for the week. In addition, you get a decent cookbook of healthy recipes. You learn about Weight Watchers, and find out where the closest one is to you, so you can go to the first meeting and sign-up. Setup a weight chart and post it on your bathroom wall. Get a decent scale that can measure weight and body fat percentage. Make a list of sample meals (breakfasts, lunches, and dinners), and post it on your refrigerator. At this point, all of this goes into the written plan.

Step Four: Then you execute — hard and fast. You can almost certainly carry out the whole plan in one day. Attend your first Weight Watchers meeting and get all the materials. Clear out the unhealthy food from the kitchen. Buy the new groceries, the new cookbook, and the new scale. Post the weight chart and the sample meals list. Select recipes and cook a batch of food for the week. By the end of the day, you have used your willpower not to diet directly but to establish the conditions that will make your diet easier to follow. When you wake up the next morning, you will find your surroundings dramatically changed in coordination with your plan. Your fridge will be stocked with plenty of pre-cooked healthy food for you to eat. You will be a member of

Weight Watchers and will have weekly gatherings to attend. You will have a routine block of time set apart for grocery shopping and food preparation. It will still require some discipline to follow your diet, but you have already changed things so much that it will not be nearly as difficult as it would be without these changes.[31]

Without self-discipline, building the life you want would only stay a dream. Whichever area of your life that needs self-discipline you need to develop it. Bear in mind that "Heights that great men reached and kept were not obtained by sudden flight but, while their companions slept, they were toiling upward in the night"[32], as Henry Wadsworth Longfellow puts it.

PART
THREE

The Real Cost of the Build to the Builder

Every great work, every great accomplishment, has been brought into manifestation through holding to the vision, and often just before the big achievement, comes apparent failure and discouragement.
- Florence Scovel Shinn

4

MANIFEST THE DESIGN OF THE ARCHITECT ON THE GROUND

The intelligent man is one who
has successfully fulfilled many
accomplishments, and is yet willing
to learn more.

-Ed Parker

Live The God-ordained Life

God teaches us through the scriptures, that even before we become human beings here on earth, He already had our lives planned out. This evidence can be picked from His discourse with the prophet

Jeremiah in chapter 1 verse 4 and 5 " *Before I formed you in the womb I knew you; Before you were born I sanctified you; I ordained you a prophet to the nations.*" Even before Jeremiah could learn to walk and talk, he had already been ordained a prophet unto the nations. The Lord has a blue print for each one of us, which many refer to as purpose and teaches us how we can live out or manifest that blue print through instructions He has made explicitly clear in the scriptures. It is not enough to say what your God-given purpose or your God-ordained life is

Let your works do the talking instead of talking so much and not accomplishing anything. The architects plan and design for our lives is what we have referred to as purpose or the God-ordained life. The God-ordained life is like a plan of a building, the magnificence is not what remains on the paper but in the physical construction. Many have abandoned the process of accomplishing or manifesting the design of the architect of our lives altogether because they were confronted with challenges. Others cannot simply figure out what this ordained life is, but if you have been reading this book from the beginning you should by now understand this concept quite well.

You Are Unique Through And Through

You are not 'you' until you manifest your God-ordained life. It is just like handing over the contract of the building of your physical house to a contractor only to find out after completion that what he or she has built - although it is a building does not match the plan and design. We need to understand that we stand out from the over 6 billion people on earth not only with our fingerprint or with DNA but also with the life God has ordained for us. No two lives are the same; you are unique more than you are aware. You need to start living off that life God has ordained for you now. You should not waste any more time. You are faced with many obstacles but there is no doubt that, whatsoever is born of God overcomes the world even our faith (see 1 John 5:4). Your God-ordained life will prevail over every situation of adversity.

Let us consider this question "if your life were a building, would it have character? What does it mean to say a building has character? Join me as we explore the need to develop this concept.

Show Character in Manifesting the Design of the Architect

This is not about behavioural patterns or moral attributes, but in strength of mind, resolution and individuality - simply the qualities that distinguish an individual from another.

I have watched some games of the English Premier League where the eventual winner had to fight from being a goal down. During interviews the expression 'the boys showed great character in the game' meaning the players exhibited qualities in the game that distinguished them from the losing team. There are many daytime property shows on British Television channels where people would say 'this building has a lot of character to it', meaning there is something about the property that makes it distinctive.

Everything we construct in life must have character with it, if it is going to be pleasing to people. To manifest your God-ordained life, we need to show character, that is to say, fight to stay distinctive. In addition, this means overcoming obstacles and elements within our environment that seek to diminish our distinctiveness.

You Have Been Wired To Overcome

For everything God created, an element within it makes it able to resist and survive the hardship of its environment, even when everything else is facing the threat of destruction. For instance, in plants, there are some, which are fire resistant like the teak; there are drought resistant plants like the cactus, which grows in deserts and many more. In animals, there is mimicry. A mimic is any species that has evolved to appear similar to another species in order to dupe predators into avoiding the mimic, or dupe a prey into approaching the mimic.

Humans are not exempt from this ability given by God. There was one man in scripture that showed character in his life, Joseph, the Patriarch (see Genesis 37 -50). This man fought against all odds to become what God had ordained, he should become. The dream he had of the moon, sun and eleven stars bowing before him indeed happened, but before then there were many obstacles and various types of adversities, he had to battle challenges including being falsely accused by Portiphar's wife and was thrown into prison. There are things that Joseph did that helped him to show character.

How Joseph Exhibited Character

Guide One: Do Not Let Your Dreams Dissolve

Every individual's dream is what gives him or her reason for living. It is dreams that inspire people to live in a certain way. A person without a dream is like a plant without sunlight. Do not abandon your dreams due to challenges. Remember there are people who are depending on your dreams, visions or God-ordained life, to accomplish theirs so do not let them down. The only person who can dissolve your dreams is you. Keep your eye on what God has ordained for you. It will not fail if you can cooperate with God. You will come through if only you can keep your eye on what God has ordained for you. Keeping focus will produce the energy to manifest the life ordained by God for you.

It is You and Not Challenges That Can Dissolve Your Dreams

There is no external heat produced by the fires of life that can dissolve a dream. Joseph held onto his dreams and saw his parents and siblings come to the land where he had been elevated to become second only to the King in authority to find food. Once God placed the dream in your heart, it will surely happen right before your eyes. This is what Numbers 23:19 has to say; *"God is not a man, that He should lie, nor a son of man, that He should repent. Has He said, and will He not do? Alternatively, has He spoken, and will He not make it good?"*

Guide Two: Do not Bow to Bitterness

But now, do not therefore be grieved or angry with yourselves because you sold me here; for God sent me before you to preserve life. (Genesis 45:5)

Bitterness develops when pain or suffering which is purported to have been caused by another is unattended to. There is often an exhibition of intense animosity marked by cynicism and rancour. Have you ever been hurt by someone you love? Can you quantify the magnitude of betrayal you felt? Indeed many things potentially can make us feel bitter. I read somewhere not long ago about a woman whose son was murdered by yobs in the street. The woman said there was no way she was going to forgive the assailants. Apparently, they had taken her only child and surviving relative. Can you imagine the intensity of this woman's pain? You may be reading this book and can immediately identify with this woman's story, maybe not exactly the same, but you are nursing an intense pain that has made you extremely bitter.

Before you feel I am judging you, it is not wrong to feel hurt, but how you deal with it makes all the difference in what happens to you. There is a consequence of having bitterness in our hearts toward another although we may be justified because people might have done wrong against us. If you can forgive those who might have caused you pain you are on the way to good health and a deeper relationship with God. This would also demonstrate how deep your faith is, in God. From the scripture quoted above about Joseph, he saw the plan of God in the whole conspiracy to sell him into slavery. His brothers meant it for evil but God meant it for good. He chose to see God working through his brothers other than seeing their wickedness and hatred. Whatever you are going through right now, choose to see God working in the situation for your good other than the conspiracy of men to destroy you.

Your Bitterness May Be Justifiable But Don't Accept It

Bitterness troubles and defiles. People have developed all kinds of attitudes that repudiate those who come close to them. They are giving no one a chance into their lives to avoid being hurt again. Bitterness defiles, it conditions the heart wrongly, and as the scripture says "...God shows Himself strong on behalf of those whose heart is perfect towards Him" (2 Chronicles 16:9).

What I have come to realise in my own personal experience is that as you carry a heavy painful heart, the person or people who caused you pain do not even care about you or sometimes do not even realize what they have done to you. You want God to smile on you, take care of what concerns you, commit it to him and move on. There is no need to carry it in your heart. The problem is that sometimes we feel God will not deal with those who hurt us and cause us pain the way they deserve. The truth is, He is a just God, and we cannot fault him on how He deals with persons who go round hurting people. Choose your reaction to situations and do not allow others impose on you how you react to situations. By responding to them the way they want you to, you are no longer living your life but theirs.

Are You Bitter?

The **Bitterness Check** provided below should help you arrive at an answer.

Check One: A bitter person cares very little for the person against whom they are bitter. One of the fruits of bitterness is malice, which is a secret desire to see another suffer. Do you sometimes say 'Oh I am not hurt, I cannot be bothered…?' Yet we desire that some evil would befall those who hurt us, as a way of learning their lesson.

Check Two: A bitter person can be ungrateful. You would make light of anything and not give honour where honour is due. You may think others have not cared enough to deserve praise, even though they may not have caused you pain.

Check Three: A bitter person will help no one or complain sometimes when asked to help. You feel resentment towards everyone because you have not received justice against the one who caused you the pain. At this stage we sometimes drop out of groups where we are members and just do not want to have anything to do with people.

Check Four: A bitter person will sometimes pass cynical and harsh criticism without any legitimate reason. You just want a way to settle scores for the hurt and pain you bear. Beyond this point, we feel disliked by the group within which we find ourselves.

These points may not be exhaustive in themselves, but if you have bitterness towards someone, you know. Take steps today to forgive that person. Do not allow yourself to carry the burdens of being a prison with prisoners. Release out of your heart anyone who has caused you some form of pain. Pray that God help you deal with pain and forgive. When you forgive those who hurt you, you attract the favour and power of God. It is possible with God, if you will commit yourself and the pain to Him. When you have prayed act immediately to forgive all those you consider to have hurt you one way or the other. Joseph remarked 'you meant it for evil, against me but God meant it for good...." (Genesis 50:20)

Guide Three: Don't demand to Understand

It is intriguing that when Joseph received the promise, he did not know of any situation arising that could send him to a foreign land and be imprisoned based on a false accusation. He should be asking questions to understand why God had shown him one thing and another was happening to him. From a personal experience, it is when you demand to understand that you seem to lose faith in God. There is never going to be a time when we would fully understand the ways of God with his people. From such a comfortable life as a father's favourite to a slave boy is not understandable. If you were reading Joseph's story for the very first time, you would think God has failed him but all that he experienced was exactly what God wanted him to endure. Joseph trusted God so much that irrespective of what he had to go through; he will end up in a position where his family would bow to him. Eventually, this materialised, is not God a master artisan? You may be going through some hard times right now, and cannot understand why, but the master artisan is at work trust him to do what he has promised. If you quit demanding to understand and depend on His grace to see you through you will see the manifestation of His design for your life.

Guide Four: Do Not Fail to be Faithful

So it was, as she spoke to Joseph day by day, that he did not heed her, to lie with her or to be with her.

But it happened about this time, when Joseph went into the house to do his work, and none of the men of the house was inside, that she caught him by his garment, saying, "Lie with me." But he left his garment in her hand, and fled and ran outside.

And so it was, when she saw that he had left his garment in her hand and fled outside, that she called to the men of her house and spoke to them, saying, "See, he has brought in to us a Hebrew to mock us. He came in to me to lie with me, and I cried out with a loud voice. And it happened, when he heard that I lifted my voice and cried out, that he left his garment with me, and fled and went outside." So she kept his garment with her until his master came home. Then she spoke to him with words like these, saying, "The Hebrew servant whom you brought to us came in to me to mock me; so it happened, as I lifted my voice and cried out, that he left his garment with me and fled outside." (Genesis 39:10-18)

There are times we are tempted to take short cuts to the destination God has promised us. Think about this for a moment, that in human thinking Joseph would have wielded even more authority if he had slept with Portiphar's wife. In spite of the fact that no animosity is recorded to have been between Joseph and his master, a slave is a slave and will not enjoy the full privileges of the house in which he serves. On the other hand, he could have also used the opportunity to sleep with her as a way of getting back at his master. Even better, he would have also taken advantage of the fact that his master's house was prospering because of him. Nonetheless, he remained faithful and did not think it was payday for all his efforts and hard work. Joseph considered first the act of taking Portiphar's wife as a sin against God and secondly as a gesture of ungratefulness against Portiphar. The fear of God prevented him from committing an abominable act against the 'dream giver', God. It was not the terror of being punished by God, that bothered him but reverence for him. Here is a good description;

Therefore, since we are receiving a kingdom which cannot be shaken, let us have grace, by which we may serve God acceptably with reverence and godly fear. For our God is a consuming fire. (Hebrews 12:28-29)

Your Reverence for God Would Be A Motivation to Be Faithful

This reverence and awe motivated Joseph to surrender the desires of his flesh and the pride of having everything in Portiphar's house including his wife to God.

Joseph was a very smart person by far in today's standards. A man who could make such a crucial decision within a matter of seconds on his feet to refuse what was a tantalising offer. Proverbs 1:7 declares, "The fear of the LORD is the beginning of knowledge, But fools despise wisdom and instruction." Joseph was wise. Until we develop a reverential fear of Him, we cannot have true wisdom. Joseph could stand in faithfulness to God; he loved God and did not consider his own gratification more important. The question is how a person can be faithful to God when his own gratification means more to him than pleasing God. If we can remain faithful, God can do so much more with us. What He would do in us and through us is far more than we can do ourselves through self-gratification. Maybe you work for a company, or taking care of another's property, take good care of it, as it is through your faithfulness that God would let you have yours.

Guide Five: Do not Be Unwilling to Wait

But remember me when it is well with you, and please show kindness to me; make mention of me to Pharaoh, and get me out of this house. For indeed I was stolen away from the land of the Hebrews; and also I have done nothing here that they should put me into the dungeon." When the chief baker saw that the interpretation was good, he said to Joseph, "I also was in my dream, and there were three white baskets on my head. (Genesis 40:14-16)

The period of waiting is one of the difficult times anyone has to endure, especially when you feel time is against you. Some of us can testify at one point in our lives or the other that we had to wait on Him to deliver what He promised. When I was, little we had a mango tree behind our house and when it was the season for mangoes, I could mark out a few mangoes on the tree and check on every morning to be sure they were ripe. The reason is that the other children in the house, and I were not allowed to eat them, until they were properly ripened. Accordingly, we would wake up from bed and go straight to check whether those mangoes were ready to be plucked. These days could be indeed endless, because you also want to prevent other passers by from plucking it.

Your Time Will Come

There are situations in life where you feel you must do something quick to get what God says He has for you so others do not chance upon it or get ahead of you. The God ordained life is as an assignment handed down to you by God and providing you with tools with which you can accomplish the assignment. He cannot give you an assignment and not give you the tools to accomplish them, let alone allow others to crowd you out with the use of those tools. Some say 'God, I'm growing old, and if it has to be done it has to be now'.

Joseph had been in prison and had offered service to two men, interpreting their dreams for them. He actually told them to mention him to pharaoh, but they forgot. He had to wait on the Lord for his timing.

God Haven't Forgotten About You

We all have our periods and times within which the promises of God would be manifest. The difficult aspect of the waiting is that our timings and seasons may not just be the same on God's calendar. What we see in this story of Joseph is an incredible ability to wait for God's timing. You may have a circle of friends where every one of them may seem to be coming into their God-ordained life. Their direction in life seems to be taking on meaning whilst you appear stuck in one place without any progression of some sort. You have started questioning the ability of God to bring to pass what He has aforementioned He will do in your life. In the end, the person whom Joseph told to speak of him to the king forgot about his promise to make mention of him to the king. As if forgotten Pharaoh one day had a dream that he could not remember or interpret, and it was at that point that the former prisoner reminisced and mentioned him to the king. This placed him right in the centre of God's will. There is no cause to fear, because faithful is He who has called you. He will execute in your life what He has ordained for you. We would consider another character in the Bible – David, in a similar vein.

David: From The Desert To The Palace

We would examine a scripture below from

which vital lessons from the life of David is drawn, as we learn about how to manifest the plan and design of the architect for our lives.

And Samuel said to Jesse, "Are all the young men here?" Then he said, "There remains yet the youngest, and there he is, keeping the sheep." And Samuel said to Jesse, "Send and bring him. For we will not sit down till he comes here." So he sent and brought him in. Now he was ruddy, with bright eyes, and good-looking. And the LORD said, "Arise, anoint him; for this is the one!" Then Samuel took the horn of oil and anointed him in the midst of his brothers; and the Spirit of the LORD came upon David from that day forward. So Samuel arose and went to Ramah. (1 Samuel 16:11-13)

So it was, when the Philistine arose and came and drew near to meet David, that David hurried and ran toward the army to meet the Philistine. Then David put his hand in his bag and took out a stone; and he slung it and struck the Philistine in his forehead, so that the stone sank into his forehead, and he fell on his face to the earth. So David prevailed over the Philistine with a sling and a stone, and struck the Philistine and killed him. But there was no sword in the hand of David. Therefore David ran and stood over the Philistine, took his sword and drew it out of its sheath and killed him, and cut off his head with it. And when the Philistines saw that their champion was dead, they fled.(1 Samuel 17:48-51)

David is anointed as king to succeed Saul but not as someone who slings stones; however, it was the slinging of stones as a core skill or capability that got him into the public eye. And in due course into the palace to manifest his ordained life. There is no clear relationship between slinging stones and reigning as king, however stone slinging for David was the skill and capability, which became the vehicle to the throne. David used his time in the wilderness as a shepherd to develop and perfect his skill of stone slinging. From David's own submission, it is possible he did not deliberately learn the skill however; it became the only means ready for him to use, to drive away wild creatures who wanted to prey on the flock in his care. Whatsoever the premise of his skill development and perfection was, this skill had nothing to do with David reigning as king. The motivating force behind the stone slinging in itself has a connection to being king, since as a king you would have guardianship for your people.

Add Value to Yourself Even In Your Obscurity

There are skills that you have that situations in life might have controlled you to develop without even knowing what it could do for you in future. This reminds one of the assurances of the encompassing love of God, stated in Romans 8:28. You may not exactly know what gains you are making in the situation you find yourself in right now, so do not totally dismiss your situation as useless. Know also that you may have some skills which you cannot really link up with what you know is your God-ordained life, but it is worth developing it and become a master of it.

From inference of the scriptures about David, he had other attitudes chaperoned with the stone slinging that made it relevant to his God-ordained life. A skill without the right attitude is wasted.

Sharpen Your Skill to Make it Relevant to Your God-ordained Life

Skill Sharpening Technique One:

Have An Absolute Love for God and His People

The expression of David's love for God evident in the statement he made in, 1 Samuel 17:26 "Then David spoke to the men who stood by him, saying, "What shall be done for the man who kills this Philistine and takes away the reproach from Israel? For who is this uncircumcised Philistine, that he should defy the armies of the living God?" He thought about the name of the Lord being blasphemed by someone who has no experience of God's power as he had in the wilderness, where He overpowered a lion and a bear by the power of God. He also felt that potentially, the people of Israel had been psychologically programmed to feel inferior to their enemy. After all, they were the army of the Living God. This is a pure love he had for God and Israel that might only have been developed and cultivated in the wilderness. He just could not stand seeing someone talk about what he or she did not know and had not experienced. He took the opportunity out of the sight of men or the lime light to develop a strong relationship with a tried and tested God. Therefore, he was convinced beyond every shadow of doubt that God and his people were bigger than the challenge ahead of them. When you have known God and have walked with God, and can attest of His awesomeness, it is heartbreaking or hear comments from people who do not have any personal experience with His power and love.

Love for God Demands Everything

During Jesus' time on earth the Jewish religion, Judaism placed many obligations or prerequisites on the Jews. These obligations or commandments came from the Mosaic Law and the teachings of the prophets. Jesus summed up all these laws to make it comprehensible and simple by explaining that there are only two basic commandments from God.

"Teacher, which is the great commandment in the law?"
Jesus said to him, " 'You shall love the LORD your God

with all your heart, with all your soul, and with all your mind.' This is the first and great commandment. And the second is like it: 'You shall love your neighbor as yourself.' On these two commandments hang all the Law and the Prophets."(Matthew 22:36-40)

What does it mean to love God as expressed in Jesus' words?

Jesus taught us a few ways to express and demonstrate our love for God:

Demonstration One: Place God Above all Else In Your Life

As seen from the previous chapter, there is nothing wrong with owning physical possessions or the things we need, it is only when we make it our prime occupation - chasing after wealth as if that is all that matters in life – that God frowns on it. Our modern society seems to have reduced success to having wealth. Wealth indeed is important because those who pass it on as inheritance are referred to as good men, so there is nothing wrong about owning it. It is when it takes the place of God in our lives. People would wake up without making time with God. The ironic thing is this 'good' wealth comes to those who first seek God and there is no sorrow added to it, because technology has provided such an abundance of consumer products, the quest for these consumer products may even be a stronger temptation in our time. We may work long hours with overtime at stressful jobs, so we can acquire countless consumer products including luxury cars and other designer range of products. All these are legitimate if only these hours do not keep us away from God and the work of the Kingdom. See how the rich young ruler represents many of us in the verses below;

Now as He was going out on the road, one came running, knelt before Him, and asked Him, "Good Teacher, what shall I do that I may inherit eternal life?"
So Jesus said to him, "Why do you call Me good? No one is good but One, that is, God. You know the commandments: 'Do not commit adultery,' 'Do not murder,' 'Do not steal,' 'Do not bear false witness,' 'Do not defraud,' 'Honor your father and your mother.'"
And he answered and said to Him, "Teacher, all these things I have kept from my youth."
Then Jesus, looking at him, loved him, and said to him, "One thing you lack: Go your way, sell whatever you have and give to the poor, and you will have treasure in heaven; and come, take up the cross, and follow Me."
But he was sad at this word, and went away sorrowful, for he had great possessions.
Then Jesus looked around and said to His disciples, "How hard it is for those who have riches to enter the kingdom of God!" And the disciples were astonished at His words. But Jesus answered again and said to them, "Children, how hard it is for those who trust in riches to

enter the kingdom of God! It is easier for a camel to go through the eye of a needle than for a rich man to enter the kingdom of God."(Mark 10:17-25)

Do not condemn yourself Just Yet!

Jesus did not condemn the man's wealth but found he was obsessed with it and so when asked to go and sell them and give them to the poor, he left and did not return to Jesus. It is for this reason that many of us cannot even pay our tithe and give any good offerings unto God, but David was different:

"Then the king said to Araunah, "No, but I will surely buy it from you for a price; nor will I offer burnt offerings to the LORD my God with that which costs me nothing." So David bought the threshing floor and the oxen for fifty shekels of silver". (2 Samuel 24:24)

I would often tell people at premarital counselling that one of the things to find out is whether your prospective spouse fears and loves God enough to pay their tithe. The reason is if an individual can rob God, he or she will not place any value on you either. Often the humour with which I share this makes us all giggle, but it is no trivial issue. If this individual cannot love his or her creator, do you think he or she can be sincere about his love for you? It is what you place value on that you esteem highly. I am sharing this on the basis that tithe and other commitments to the kingdom of God is done out of a deep sincere love for God and not a mere ritual.

Demonstration Two: Live With Humility

David's humility was remarkable, because he credited everything he had as a gift from God. We are God's children and we should show Him our impeccable faith and trust. He learnt to bring the combat to the doorstep of God and not carry it, himself. His humility was premised on his love for God and his people. When confronted by his brothers about being imperious, he expressed his humility in declaring there is a cause for a man to show up for God.

Now Eliab his oldest brother heard when he spoke to the men; and Eliab's anger was aroused against David, and he said, "Why did you come down here? And with whom have you left those few sheep in the wilderness? I know your pride and the insolence of your heart, for you have come down to see the battle." And David said, "What have I done now? Is there not a cause?"(1 Samuel 17:28-29)

Qualify Yourself For Exaltation

A man God can use to bring about the deliverance of His people must have humility. Humility is the exact opposite of being boastful, arrogant and aggressive without substance. Humility diminishes when we start comparing our strengths to the weaknesses of others. In this instance of the scripture, David sought to elevate the power of God above his own. It is best if God exalts us, then He will take care of what it takes to remain there, but if on the contrary we exalt ourselves without His help, we have to device means to sustain ourselves up there. Let people think you are stupid and nothing but a doormat, the day of reckoning is near, when they would be proven wrong. You will be exalted before their eyes. There is no doubt we are all presented with the opportunities before our time and season and David's brothers thought it was one such moment for David. They were proven wrong because what ensued later exonerated him.

But he who is greatest among you shall be your servant. And whoever exalts himself will be humbled, and he who humbles himself will be exalted.(Matthew 23:11-12)

Let God Exalt You Rather Than Exalt Yourself.

Check your heart for the motive for every undertaking, is it to raise the name of the Lord and draw men to Him or for your self-gratification. Many walk about today in the church without knowing they are prideful. The walk with God is not a sprint race, it is a race undertaken with a stride at a time. Let God be exalted in your life and let people attribute to him your success. The one who would manifest his or her God – ordained life in its fullness are the ones who humble themselves.

Skill Sharpening Two: Stay committed to God and His Kingdom

Jesus is our example of a person who was totally committed to fulfilling His earthly mission. Likewise, He expects us to demonstrate the same level of total, passionate commitment to our calling whatever it might be. In spite of the fact that we might need to be able to fully live up to Jesus' example, we can definitely do our best to live off our faith every second, minute and hour of the day.

It is of utmost importance to remember, that what we commit ourselves to, is not our own agenda but Christ's. By now, we understand that there is the need to find out what is important to God and His kingdom and align what is important to us in order to please Him. We demonstrate our love for God when we forsake all our conveniences and advantages to follow the will of our Lord. The love of God for humankind is to give His only begotten son to die. It is right to say then; we can demonstrate our love for God when we die, a little, each day for His course. Dying a little may mean little sacrifices you make for the sake of Christ.

Take Good Care Of Another's

Being in the wilderness, David showed his commitment of taking care of his father's flock as if it was his own. I am not sure how much direct benefit, he would have got from that assignment, but it was an assignment well executed. When a lion and a bear would attack the flock, he killed them and delivered the flock. Like David you may have been dumped in your wilderness and been assigned some mundane task which you will benefit very little from, yet you do it with all your heart. You may be handed down a responsibility where you may think is below your capacity to perform, do not despise the responsibility, carry it out with excellence because it will magnify your skill and get you to the top.

Skill Sharpening Three: Develop Total Respect for Authority

We come to think about the fact that David did not rebel against his father bestowing him the responsibility of taking care of the flock in the wilderness. He respected his father, in our society this day law and order has broken down because our prevailing culture instructs us to esteem ourselves better than another. I have also encountered people who would respond to you with the word please and yet do not have any respect for people. Honouring and respecting people goes beyond giving verbal homage to them. It is indeed acting and living in a way that communicates to people their value to you. Now to the story of David, what would have happened if he had rebelled against his father's decision to go with the flock to look after them? The answer is obvious, he would not have had the opportunity to perfect his skill of stone slinging, which eventually became the tool with which he defeated Goliath.

Respect People Too

Irrespective of the age of an individual who is over us, at church, workplace, school etc, we need to respect them. People are fond of comparing themselves to others mismatching their strengths to their weaknesses and tend to dismiss others and deprive them the respect they deserve. Remember they are not in authority by themselves God placed them there.

Let every soul be subject to the governing authorities. For there is no authority except from God, and the authorities that exist are appointed by God. (Romans 13:1)

It is not important how smart you consider yourself to be and the capabilities you have, once you have someone else above you either in rank etc you will need to give them their due respect. Not only did David respect authority, he generally respected people for who they are.

Let every soul be subject to the governing authorities. For there is no authority except from God, and the authorities that exist are appointed by God.(2 Samuel 23:16-17)

The reason David did not drink the water was that he felt they had risked too much for him, because he valued them so much. He appreciated their efforts, but felt God deserved that honour and respect. David's respect for authority was demonstrated at a time when Saul was pursuing him to kill him; he exhibited once again his respect for a man placed in authority by God. In the case of David and Saul, both knew the one whom God had chosen was the former and yet decided not to take the place of God but rather, leave Him to deal with Saul Himself.

And he said to his men, "The LORD forbid that I should do this thing to my master, the LORD's anointed, to stretch out my hand against him, seeing he is the anointed of the LORD."(1 Samuel 24:5-6)

Skill Sharpening Four: Endeavour To Depend on God's Ability

David was a man who trusted in God's ability and not his. You would think that after gaining such a mastery of his skill, he would be confident in his ability to use the sling to kill Goliath instead he trusted in the Lord who delivered him from the lion and the bear. There is never going to be a time when our ability is going to be enough to manifest fully our God-ordained life, we need the strength of God. It is easy to attribute our success at the various stages of life to our skills due to our physical involvement. It is a privilege for God to ask us for involvement in manifesting the total plan for our lives. We must learn to give him the glory and not take it, because His glory, He will share with no one. Our ability is limited but God's is infinite. When we are tired, He is strong, when we are about to give up, He is getting ready to give His best. You can trust in God's ability to help you manifest His ordained life for you. You would realise that when an architect makes his drawings of a building, he gives it to builders to translate what is on the paper into real physical terms. As part of the process, he often pays visits to the site to make sure what is presented in the plans is being followed. The builder no matter how good he or she is must submit to the one who made the design and cooperate to make the building project a success.

Our relationship with God as the architect goes beyond thee scenario above. He is on the site with us all the time, and does the job with us on day-to-day basis. If we can only trust in his ability to use whatever skills we have to accomplish the building of the design it would be an understatement to say we will be successful. Our skills have an edge when He is in control. This however does not exempt us from gaining mastery of our skills, because David was a master of stone slinging. He killed a lion and a bear and Goliath with it. There is a process required for any individual to go through to gain mastery.

The Process of Mastery of Core Skills and or Core Capabilities

In the context of David's story mastery is what you learn and become in the process of manifesting the architect's plan and design or His ordained life for you. The manifestation process involves the acquisition and creation of tangible material things and assets which can be lost through fire, theft etc. If you have mastered the skills that were the vehicle for manifesting the architect's design for your life, it is possible you can replicate and reproduce it again.

Mastery Process One: You Must Develop Strength To Seize Your Moment

In the United States for instance, it is found that 81 per cent of millionaire lottery winners file for bankruptcy within 5 years of winning[33]. Most of them have not yet mastered the millionaire lifestyle and pattern of thinking. In short, they do not have what it takes to maintain and even increase what they have, so they eventually lose it.

Most successful companies, nations and individuals have core competencies, which I have referred to as core skills and capabilities. This is simply an area of expertise that others would find difficult to imitate. One thing about core competencies is that it has a breath of application to a wide variety of areas[34] in manifesting our God-ordained life. The main skill that you possess gives you an advantage in your field of endeavour and in life in general. The stone slinging was the core skill that David possessed which now of facing Goliath, gave him an advantage over him. The skill distinguished him from the rest of the men in the army. You can only seize your moment when you have mastered very well your core skills and capabilities. Men who are considered successful are only playing their game with the area of their strength. There is a process to obtain the same level of proficiency in slinging stones.

Mastery Process Two: You May Spend More Time in Your Wilderness.

The wilderness is a moment in your life, where you feel you are in the middle of nowhere, far away from your dreams, visions, aspirations and the life God has ordained for you. You sometimes feel you have been locked up without a way of escape. Sometimes it feels as though it is even safer and strategically wise to hang in there because you do not know which way to turn. The message for you at this moment of your life is to continue to sharpen your skills. David took full advantage of his loneliness in the wilderness to learn, that which would in the future bring him to the throne. He understood how to trade a position of disadvantage for an advantage. He turned his bitter experience into better experience.

Your perception of the situation you find yourself in immediately would inform the actions and decisions you take. Therefore, you need to perceive right. In perceiving right you can spot an advantage in a situation of adversity. This is exactly what David did.

Prepare to Last

You may be reading this book immediately and maybe wondering why everyone seems to have gone ahead of you. People you may even consider yourself smarter than are making it big, and you cannot even have a break in your field of endeavour. Remember life is a race, but not a race where we compete against each other; instead, we strive to finish our race. It is interesting that the acorn fruit of the oak tree takes six to eighteen months to mature. This is the entire life cycle of another plant and yet just the fruit take that long to mature. No wonder the oak tree lives for a very long time. As a result, many nations including England, Estonia, France, Germany, and United

States of America among others have chosen it as the national tree. As a point of interest, another plant that the scriptures use to describe the state of the believer is the oil palm. Read it below.

The righteous shall flourish like a palm tree; He shall grow like a cedar in Lebanon. (Psalm 92:12)

The economically viable life span of an oil palm is typically around 22 to 30 years. You need to understand that there is a divine design why you are where you are right now. What you need to do is to develop any skill you have as this may prove to be very useful to see the full manifestation of your God-ordained life.

Mastery Process Three: You Will Have Very Difficult Tasks to Deal With

Hard times come to toughen us or flatten us. As part of the process of gaining mastery of your core skills and capabilities, you will be presented with instances where your present capabilities and skills would be stretched. It is when this has occurred that you can be confident that presented with a similar situation you are sure of handling it with ease. You see, God will not give you a challenge in the open if He has not already given you a similar one in secret. Even for us teachers we do not precede the introduction of new topics with examination questions. It is when a subject or topic has been taught that a test or examination can be set to assess the understanding of our students. It is for this reason the scriptures assures us in James 1:2 "My brethren, count it all joys when you fall into various trials," The difficulties will produce in you a gem that nothing else can help develop in you. David faced the lion and the bear in the wilderness, both very fearsome and fearful animals in the wild yet he killed them all alone in the wilderness. At a point in life, you will face a situation that can potentially destroy you forever, leave you with scars forever, or let you live in fear forever, or even make you hide your skills forever. For David his difficult task was the lion, the bear, and the dangers of being all alone in the wilderness. Your difficult tasks may be caring for your ailing parents, bringing up your teenage children, putting up with an unappreciative boss, or a hateful colleague at work. For whatever the situation may be, the difficult tasks are essential to the sharpening of your core skills and capabilities, which would be instrumental in manifesting the design of the architect for your life.

Your Perseverance Will Reward You

Remember to persevere because your promotion to the throne is linked with your ability to handle the difficult tasks handed down to you. You know that pastors do not preach their first sermons after being appointed pastors of a church. They do that at the seminary. Therefore, it is with every vocation or profession, caterers cook their first culinary dish at school and not at the restaurant of their first appointment. Many jobs these days advertised are searching for people with some kind of experience, it is for the employers to be sure the individual has developed or is developing the capability to handle the responsibilities that go with the position. Be patient and kill your bear and your lion and certainly God is preparing your moment with your Goliath for you. If you do well now it is likely, you will excel handling your Goliath when the time comes.

Mastery Process Four: Be Ready to Lay down Your Life

Until you have had something to die for, you will have nothing to live for. The degree to which you love the life God has ordained for you will determine the lengths you are prepared to go to see it happen. When people say I have not been praying much these days it is evidence, they have nothing to live for. Have you come to ask yourself what stimulates a person who try to jump over an obstacle, the length of about three storey buildings on a motor bike? David asked for what shall be done for the one who fight Goliath. When he was told, he saw within that promise the opportunity to change his life completely from being a shepherd boy to the son-in-law to the king of Israel. The reason God gives us glimpses of our future, His ordained life for us is to motivate us to hold on even when it is tough. In almost every area of life, our willingness to lay down our lives would distinguish us from mere achievers to good and faithful servants.

David loved his potential new life so much that he might have forgotten the dangers associated with the task he was taking upon himself. The joy of the future made him numb to the real risks of fighting a man who has been a fighter from his youth. Maybe it might have crossed his mind at a point that he was being ambitious, but for an individual who is ready to lay down his or her life, fear is not an issue.

Stick Your Head In

"looking unto Jesus, the author and finisher of our faith, who for the joy that was set before Him endured the cross, despising the shame, and has sat down at the right hand of the throne of God. For consider Him who endured such hostility from sinners against Himself, lest you become weary and discouraged in your souls. You have not yet resisted to bloodshed, striving against sin". (Hebrews 12:2-4)

He endured the cross due to the motivation of a high position in glory. If Jesus did it then we can trust God on daily basis to look beyond our moments of pain, discouragement, frustration, confusion, hopelessness and faithlessness to the exalted place in life, as we manifest the architect's design for our lives.

In a speech given in Paris at the Sorbonne in 1910, Theodore Roosevelt said, "it is not the critic who counts, not the man who points out how the strongmen stumbled or where the doer of deeds could have done better. The credit belongs to the man who is actually in the arena, whose face is marred by dust and sweat and blood, who strives valiantly, who errs and comes short again and again, who knows the great enthusiasms, the great devotions and spends himself in a worthy cause. Who at best knows achievement and who at the worst fails whilst daring greatly so that his place shall never be with those cold and timid souls who neither saw victory nor defeat"[35]. There is no question about 'what if I give my all and it fails?' At least you tried. Furthermore, many who try have made something extraordinary out of their lives.

You can only lay down your life for what you shall become. Every great achievement has been preceded by a great sacrifice. Step out of your boat today unto the water like Apostle Peter did, you will not fail, do not let the fear of the unknown cripple you. David knew Goliath's credentials and yet he let the reward motivate him to victory. Your victory is at hand, if only you sacrifice a little, risk your life for what you want.

Mastery Process Five: Your Intentions Would Be Misjudged

For every individual who manifest his or her God-ordained life would be misjudged at one point or the other. It is very difficult to understand a person with a passion to accomplish a dream or vision. Until there is an accomplishment, it is easy to think they are even doing things over the top. It is not surprising that Peter rebuked Christ when He mentioned about His imminent death:

From that time Jesus began to show to His disciples that He must go to Jerusalem, and suffer many things from the elders and chief priests and scribes, and be killed, and be raised the third day. Then Peter took Him aside and began to rebuke Him, saying, "Far be it from You, Lord; this shall not happen to You!" But He turned and said to Peter, "Get behind Me, Satan! You are an offense to Me, for you are not mindful of the things of God, but the things of men."
(Matthew 16:21-23)

Christ knew what He was on earth to do and had the passion to accomplish it and no one would stand in His way. David's experience was no different; his brothers to whom he was delivering supplies, thought he had come to the battleground at his own behest. Whilst there, the champion of Gath, Goliath appears and makes his boasting. It was at this time that David said 'is there not a cause?' David saw the opportunity for his upliftment to the throne his brothers were seeing pride. It is not always important what men perceive you to be, it is your motive and condition of your heart that matters.

Humans would have their own perceptions about you, even when you are convicted to be wrong in your heart, some would perceive you are right and vice versa. Every person you can count on as mentor or look up to would tell you, of having had his or her intentions misjudged before. Being misjudged is part of the process of gaining mastery of the skills that would take you to the top of manifesting your God-ordained life. We are sometimes too concerned about what people say about us and as a result, we are not able to follow our convictions. The truth is this; every individual has a course to chart, given by God. There is no way people are going to fully understand you and appreciate where you are going. You only need to be strong, and keep your head up high, with the design of the architect in focus. Refuse to be distracted and reject the men-pleasing game. It is your destiny. Your judges will come to understand you later.

Mastery Process Six: Your Opportunity Would Wait Until You Have Mastered Your Core Skill and Capability

Opportunities come and go and it is those who are prepared who take full advantage of them. Until an individual has mastered his or her skill, it is difficult to identify an opportunity in the first place. Have you ever been in a situation where you starred in the face of a potential opportunity to go by, because you did not seem to be ready yet? You can only access your opportunity if and only if you have mastered your core skills and capabilities, Goliath had been terrorizing the people of Israel for two weeks, and twice each day before David visited his brothers in the camp. If David did not have the skills to match the challenge, it could have gone on for month's even years until someone was ready to face Goliath. Everyone needs an opportunity to prove the worth of his or her skills. Until Goliath appeared, it is not clear how David could have used his core skill to get to the throne eventually. He killed Goliath with the slinging of the stone and immediately gained national support to be the legitimate leader of God's people. The people had found someone who they thought could lead them in tough times.

Keep Working On Yourself

The saddest thing to happen to any individual is for him or her to miss an opportunity because they were unprepared to take it up. The fact that what you are looking out for as an opportunity has not come, means that your preparation is not yet complete. In other words, you have not mastered yet your core skills. Spend time and continue to work on your core skills. Keep working on it; mastering it. Because given the opportunity, they would blow it. You may be aware that there are various agencies who 'head hunt' for positions in big firms. Being head hunted is because the demand for them is high because of the fact that they have really mastered their core skills and at this point they negotiate for their salaries, which is normally very high. All you need to do is to master your core skills and capabilities and wait for your opportunity.

Mastery Process Seven: No Other Skill Will Work For You Like The One you Have Mastered.

David has been accepted as the man to face Goliath, needed armour to fight according to the calculations of the army generals, and experienced military men. Saul gave David armour, but the latter could not use it because he had not tried it before. He realized that he could not depend on something that he was not used to for the needed protection. That was a wise decision, using the armour could have distracted him from using what he felt comfortable with and trusted to provide him with the desired results. We are sometimes made to feel by others as though the skills we possess are not as important as they have.

What the world has embraced as innovation has always been on the mind of - and heart of - the innovator. He has brooded upon it for days, weeks; months even years tested it and explored many ways of solving all potential problems and limitations to the product. You will have to understand that the core skill you have is linked with your ordained life and for that, matter it is not just anything you do that will get you to the throne.

This is the reason in the very first chapter we spoke about first things first. You need to have in hand the plan and design made by the architect. It is when this has been done, that the requisite tools needed, could be identified and sought for, in order to be able to build what is on the plan. In David's case, he was thrust into it without even knowing the essence of the stone slinging. The word of caution is whatever you are engaged in, do it with all your heart strength and might.

Mastery Process Eight: Your Recognition Will Only Come after You Have Mastered Your Skills

People would celebrate those who provide answers to their questions and solutions to their problems. When the skills you have mastered start affecting the lives of others, then you would have recognition. Your name would become synonymous to what you provide with your skills. The women sung songs for David because he had solved the problem of their nation. His was a man that a few months and years earlier had been in the wilderness without any hope of a better future; he swapped his feeling of abandonment with mastering a skill that would become the vehicle to the throne eventually. You will sometimes feel like an abandoned piece of scrap in a blacksmith shop but make the most out of your situation. When the black smith feels you are ready. You will be back to be shaped and displayed on the shelves. We all sometimes feel left behind, especially when we feel others are rising to their thrones ahead of us; however, we need to understand that when the time comes, it would not pass us by. We would all ascend to our thrones someday.

Before Jesus entered into Jerusalem, he asked His disciples by the gift of the word of knowledge to go to the next village, untie a colt, and bring it to Him. It was an unknown colt. What made this colt popular was the fact that Jesus sat on it. I am wondering how even the owner would treat it because as the story goes round people would want to see this colt as an evidence of Jesus' triumphant entry into Jerusalem. The colt would have just gained recognition without doing anything.

Sometimes despite all your efforts and hard work, you seem not to be recognized, it is because your time has not just come yet. Just do not go running for the recognition, it will chase after you, when you have mastered your core skills and capabilities. This should be the motivation to master whatever your core skills and capabilities may be.

Mastery of Core Skills and Capabilities Add Value to You

The process of mastery of our core skills and capabilities among other things adds value to us. In other words, it leaves us better people than before.

Added Value One: It Will Increase Your Level Of Confidence

There is two ways the process of mastery of the core skills and capabilities will create confidence; both in us and in God.

Confidence in You

You will know you have what it takes to become all that God wants you to be. This is so important considering that God cannot use a person who does not think he or she is up to the task. That belittles God's wisdom and power. God does not call the qualified he qualifies the called. He told Jeremiah that He had made him a prophet, even before he could assess his strengths and weaknesses. David's brothers misjudged his self-confidence to be pride. He had tried and tested his capability to use the sling and the stone to eliminate Goliath. The moment your confidence in your capabilities makes you feel better than others that is when pride comes in, but there is nothing wrong if you are a self-confident person. Self-confidence is an essential ingredient for success.

Remember how God used circumstances to boost Gideon's self-image. When he addressed him as a mighty man of valour (see Judges 6:12). Gideon could not believe God had chosen him to accomplish such a great task. For the lack of self- confidence, he decided to carryout part of his assignment in the night (see Judges 6:27). We have all been through situations in our lives that had diminished our self-confidence. Your economic background, the family within which you were born and sometimes-certain failures we had with some undertakings in the past.

The past is never the measure of what your future will be, it is only what you do now, that can shape your future the way you want it. Your today is a gift for you to correct the mistakes of your past by doing all that you need to do.

Confidence In God

David proved that the process of mastery of his capabilities helped him to develop confidence in God's ability. In his statements, "God had delivered a lion and a bear to him and trusted that Goliath wasn't going to be an exception to the story. It is like the story of the three Hebrew men, Shadrach, Meshach, and Abednego. They had so much trust in God that they confidently stipulated that God would deliver them.

Then Nebuchadnezzar, in rage and fury, gave the command to bring Shadrach, Meshach, and Abed-Nego. So they brought these men before the king. Nebuchadnezzar spoke, saying to them, "Is it true, Shadrach, Meshach, and Abed-Nego, that you do not serve my gods or worship the gold image which I have set up? Now if you are ready at the time you hear the sound of the horn, flute, harp, lyre, and psaltery, in symphony with all kinds of music, and you fall down and worship the image which I have made, good! But if you do not worship, you shall be cast immediately into the midst of a burning fiery furnace.

And who is the god who will deliver you from my hands?"
Shadrach, Meshach, and Abed-Nego answered and said to the king, "O Nebuchadnezzar, we have no need to answer you in this matter. (Daniel 3:13-16)

They knew their God and been through the process. In relation to the above, David's confidence was not in what he would become but in God. He relied on God, and knew that what he shall become after killing Goliath was nothing if God had not given him the opportunity. It seems to me these days that people are over-dependent on prophets and prophesies. The prophets only declare what God has revealed to them. Prophetic utterances do not fulfil themselves; neither can the prophets make it happen. God makes it happen and we should rather be God-dependent.

Many of us believe in ourselves and believe in what we shall become but not in God. We have so much confidence in what we shall become that we forget the one who would make it happen. You need to bear in mind that before there was a plan for your life, before there was a fashioning of your future, there was God. David was not the only one who had this quality about him, there are many great men including Abraham who had this quality about them.

By faith he dwelt in the land of promise as in a foreign country, dwelling in tents with Isaac and Jacob, the heirs with him of the same promise; for he waited for the city which has foundations, whose builder and maker is God. (Hebrews 11:9-10)

For Abraham to be looking out for this city, he should then know this God quite well and the usual characteristics, of His foundations and buildings. Literally speaking if you were to walk into an estate without a builders sign post, and you are able to tell who the builders are by the interior and exterior characteristics, it is very likely you are familiar with them. Surely, some sort of closeness to God is the only way that can produce the kind of convictions Abraham had of God.

Are You not our God, who drove out the inhabitants of this land before Your people Israel, and gave it to the descendants of Abraham Your friend forever?
(2 Chronicles 20:7)

Abraham is here referred to as the friend of God, closeness to God begins with closeness to His Word- the scriptures reveal the awesomeness, faithfulness, goodness, mercy of the Most High God. The Word of God reveals His involvement in our day-to-day lives, even when things are not going the way we want it.

Added Value Two: It Will Enable You To Recognize Your Opportunities

When you know what God's plan is for your life, and know what skills and capabilities you have, you can recognize when your opportunities arrive. You will be able to tell what the opportunities are and what they are not. No one had told David that his time to leave the wilderness had come in the person of Goliath. He was very well prepared for Goliath. It is for this reason that he asked what shall be done for the one who slain Goliath. After all, if there are not 'men' in Israel to fight this giant, a man of war from his youth, there should be some form of reward for whoever risks his life to face him. He knew exactly that it was time for his immediate elevation. You can call his going to the battlefield a divine coincidence, but he had also prepared to deal with the task on hand. You will know which situation and circumstances to take advantage of when you have prepared yourself. Continue preparing because your day of opportunity is close.

Added Value Three: It Will Enable You To Build Selflessness Into The Fibre Of Your Being

David was confronted with a difficult task of killing the lion and the bear; however, he was ready to put his life on the line. He had already learnt this in the wilderness; he put his life on the line for the flock he was shepherding. For no one can stop a person who is ready to die for what they believe in. After all the highest punishment, a person can suffer is death. The process of being in the wilderness all by himself to master his capabilities and skills made David selfless. When everyone else was scared, he stood up to fight. Most companies seek to hire people who can work within a team. You cannot work in a team and not be selfless for instance, because it involves sharing ideas, expertise and efforts to get an assignment accomplished. For any individual who aspires to manifest his or her God-ordained life, must develop selflessness. No accomplishment comes cheap to anyone; you will have to give up something to get something. The story of Michelangelo's painting of the ceiling of the Sistine Chapel is one typical example. He spent 4 years lying on his back this is what he had to say 'if people knew how hard I had to work to gain my mastery, it wouldn't be wonderful at all'.

Selflessness Enables You Emerge As a Leader

One of the tests of leadership is the ability to handle crisis. It seems to me most leaders emerge on the wave of a crisis or another. There is no leadership without 'follower ship' and for people to follow you they want to see the individual has distinguished himself or herself to solving their problem and providing them with the inspiration to become all they can be. The process of developing leadership in the context of David's story began in the wilderness, perhaps it is the reason he was sent into the wilderness. This was to condition him mentally to become a leader. Understand the statement that crisis is only a midwife to a leader but does not give birth to leadership. Dr. Myles Munroe writes that 'our mental conditioning determines our success or failure. You have to train to become what you want to be. The reason soldiers are sent to boot camp is to get them to stop thinking like civilians and start thinking like professionals. In boot camp they are isolated from their families and friends and rest of society so that they can focus on their new mind set'[36].

You May Have To Give Up Your Conveniences

How else would these core capabilities and skills of David have been useful except chasing after the lion and the bear? A problem had to arise which needed these mastered capabilities as an antidote or solution, thereby pushing him out of obscurity into prominence. Winston Churchill was one such leader who emerged due to the World War, a man whom many did not have much to write home about until the war. He wrote, 'I felt as if I was walking with destiny and that all my past life had been but a preparation for this hour and for this trial'[37]. A note for those of us who run away from crisis, it is a sign that we are not ready for leadership or just merely unprepared to face trials and hardship. Think about this, if God was to appear to you and told you the crisis you are facing now is going to serve as the spring board for you to leap into leadership, would you feel a bit more relaxed and thankful? You can feel that now, no need to postpone it. What you are going through is preparing the grounds for you to emerge as a leader. It may be painful, but it is all part of the process. As you master your core capabilities and skills in those circumstances, you are only on a way out to the top.

Are You Getting Value For Money?

The process of mastery of core skills and capabilities are only part of the demand on a builder in the building process. Every one who contracts an individual or a company to work on his or her building would want to get an expert to be sure they get value for money. Unfortunately, we do not in the same sense give God the value for His grace, mercy, favour, strength, wisdom His spirit and all that He does in our lives to enable us to accomplish His ordained life for us. We need to cooperate with God, at every step of the building process, so that we can complete the building project on time.

There is never going to be a time when we would say we do not need God anymore. It will be as if terminating your contract with your architect who needs to affirm what the builders are doing is in line with the set out plan. There is the probability that a builder could construct a building that may look nice in the eyes of the ordinary man, and yet be a failure in the eyes of the architect because they did not adhere to certain standards. Like a builder would engage an architect, let us involve the Lord and cooperate with him to build a solid life. That men may see and give glory to the Father in heaven (see Matthew 5:16). Doubtlessly, submit yourself thoroughly to the process, so you can manifest God's ordained life for you

5

OVERCOMING THE OBSTACLES OF THE BUILDING PROCESS

Challenges are gifts that force us to search for a new center of gravity. Don't fight them. Just find a different way to stand. **Oprah Winfrey**

If you can find a path with no obstacles, it probably doesn't lead anywhere. **-Frank A. Clark**

Success is to be measured not so much by the position that one has reached in life as by the obstacles, which he has overcome.

-Booker T. Washington

In the process of constructing a building, many potential obstacles and encumbrances can cause a delay or even cause the builders to abandon the entire project. The same is the case in life where challenges are inevitable and may at times cause discomfort for an individual. We should not be ignorant of the fact that we do not always negotiate for obstacles and hindrances but have to negotiate our way out of them.

The middle may mean many things to many people; it may include the time between your wedding day and your silver anniversary, it may be your day of enrolment into a course and the graduation, the commencement of your business and making your first £1million.

Jesus said 'No one builds a house without first counting the cost'

For which of you, intending to build a tower, does not sit down first and count the cost, whether he has enough to finish it— lest, after he has laid the foundation, and is not able to finish, all who see it begin to mock him, saying, 'This man began to build and was not able to finish' (Luke 14:28-30)

Many times, we often interpreted this scripture to fit into the subject of preparation. Even this is true, no one can prepare adequately for obstacles and obstructions, as they tend to occur unexpectedly in the construction process.

Therefore, your preparation should include preparing to deal with the unexpected.

The question would then be "how do you prepare for situations you haven't prepared to handle?" As rhetorical this question may be, the answer lies in the awareness that there are situations you would encounter you have not prepared for.

Real Success Is Measured In Relativity To The Chances Of Failure

To know that challenges are common to men and that others have managed to get over them is enough encouragement that you can get over them too. Mahatma Ghandi, Pele, Tony Blair, Oprah Winfrey, Martin Luther King Jr., Barack Obama and other successful people have one way or the other been confronted with situations that threatened the realisation of their dreams. The reason we consider them successful is not only because of their accomplishments, but also in relativity to what could have prevented them from fulfilling those dreams. That is why they are celebrated.

Obstacles, hindrances, difficulties as we may describe them are relative to an individual's peculiar life. For some, these obstacles manifest in the form of financial difficulties, delays in education, loss of a loved one, a debt, religious persecution, sickness and so on. We would examine two characters from scripture and learn some lessons to inspire us to finish our building process.

Handle The Delays in the building Process

Now when Jesus had crossed over again by boat to the other side, a great multitude gathered to Him; and He was by the sea. And behold, one of the rulers of the synagogue came, Jairus by name. And when he saw Him, he fell at His feet and begged Him earnestly, saying, "My little daughter lies at the point of death. Come and lay Your hands on her, that she may be healed, and she will live." So Jesus went with him, and a great multitude followed Him and thronged Him. Now a certain woman had a flow of blood for twelve years, and had suffered many things from many physicians. She had spent all that she had and was no better, but rather grew worse. When she heard about Jesus, she came behind Him in the crowd and touched His garment. For she said, "If only I may touch His clothes, I shall be made well." Immediately the fountain of her blood was dried up, and she felt in her body that she was healed of the affliction. And Jesus, immediately knowing in Himself that power had gone out of Him, turned around in the crowd and said, "Who touched My clothes?" But His disciples said to Him, "You see the multitude thronging You, and You say, 'Who touched Me?'" And He looked around to see her who had done this thing. But the woman, fearing and trembling, knowing what had happened to her, came and fell down before Him and told Him the whole truth. And He said to her, "Daughter, your faith has made you well. Go in peace, and be healed of your affliction."

While He was still speaking, some came from the ruler of the synagogue's house who said, "Your daughter is dead. Why trouble the Teacher any further?"

As soon as Jesus heard the word that was spoken, He said to the ruler of the synagogue, "Do not be afraid; only believe." And He permitted no one to follow Him except Peter, James, and John the brother of James. Then He came to the house of the ruler of the synagogue, and saw a tumult and those who wept and wailed loudly. When He came in, He said to them, "Why make this commotion and weep? The child is not dead, but sleeping."

And they ridiculed Him. But when He had put them all outside, He took the father and the mother of the child, and those who were with Him, and entered where the child was lying. Then He took the child by the hand, and said to her, "Talitha, cumi," which is translated, "Little girl, I say to you, arise." Immediately the girl arose and walked, for she was twelve years of age. And they were overcome with great amazement. But He commanded them strictly that no one should know it, and said that something should be given her to eat.(Mark 5:22-43)

The ruler of the synagogue managed to take Jesus away from the crowd, who had been listening to Him. It was a great achievement, to have Jesus accompany Him to His house. One cannot possibly imagine the reaction of the crowd at the time. Perhaps, there were other sick people among the crowd probably waiting for Jesus to finish speaking and call the sick to pray for them.

The fact that Jesus left the crowd behind means that there should have been something special about this ruler of the synagogue. The only thing that comes to mind is the ruler sacrificing his position and social status to be a reproach in the eyes of the leaders and followers of Judaism at the time. This is the case because Judaism regarded Jesus and his followers as blasphemers and the entire group as a sect. It was therefore a great sacrifice on the ruler's part to publicly fall at Jesus' feet.

Obstructions Come, But The Difference Is With Whom You Are Walking

Whilst Jesus was on the way to the ruler's house, there was a sudden interruption at least in the ruler's opinion. A woman with an issue of blood touched the hem of Jesus' garment and was healed. At this point Jesus stops and asks who touched Him. This dialogue takes some precious time off the time the ruler needed to cover the distance left to reach his house for Jesus to pray for his daughter. Then a servant from his house announces his daughter has died.

There are times when we start life's building process quite well but somewhere in the process, we experience interruptions. Some of these are at times extremely threatening. You might have started a business, which has been doing very well until something just happens, and you are no longer sure whether your business can rise again.

You may have begun your family well until there was a divorce and now your once obedient, adorable children have joined drug dealing gangs you may be wondering whether these children can leave the gangs and embrace the virtues you have taught them.

Believe That Somehow You Will Overcome

This story can almost apply to every area of life when there are sudden delays that are inimical to our life's goals or life itself.

Jesus' response to the news from the ruler's house was very timely because by now the ruler's faith had sunk so low and thinking his efforts had all been in vain. He might have begun playing the blame game; complaining about the woman with the issue of blood and those who took part in the dialogue with Jesus, looking for the one who touched Jesus' garment.

Jesus turned to the ruler and said "... if only you can believe..." Whatever the middle may be to you, when

Jesus steps in, it will be a different story.

We have to believe that God can turn our circumstances around, even if they look dead. They would come back to life again. Jesus assisted the ruler to keep up his faith for the miracle that was going to take place; you need to keep up your faith to experience that miracle. You will surely finish anything you have started. There is no time too late for Jesus to come in, only believe.

Jesus Had A Middle to Deal With Too.

We have no excuse to whine or give up when we are faced with "the middle", considering that our Lord went through it. For this reason, we are told to look up to Jesus, the author and finisher of our faith. (See Hebrews 12:2).

From Jesus' birth through the time He ascended into heaven, we could find three points He reached in His life that characterizes the middle; the wilderness, the garden and the cross. We will discuss each of these points one by one.

Point One: The Wilderness

Then Jesus, being filled with the Holy Spirit, returned from the Jordan and was led by the Spirit into the wilderness, being tempted for forty days by the devil. And in those days He ate nothing, and afterward, when they had ended, He was hungry. And the devil said to Him, "If You are the Son of God, command this stone to become bread." But Jesus answered him, saying, "It is written, 'Man shall not live by bread alone, but by every word of God.'" Then the devil, taking Him up on a high mountain, showed Him all the kingdoms of the world in a moment of time. And the devil said to Him, "All this authority I will give You, and their glory; for this has been delivered to me, and I give it to whomever I wish. Therefore, if You will worship before me, all will be Yours." And Jesus answered and said to him, "Get behind Me, Satan! For it is written, 'You shall worship the LORD your God, and Him only you shall serve.'" Then he brought Him to Jerusalem, set Him on the pinnacle of the temple, and said to Him, "If you are the Son of God, throw Yourself down from here. For it is written: ' He shall give His angels charge over you, To keep you, and,' In their hands they shall bear you up, Lest you dash your foot against a stone.'" And Jesus answered and said to him, "It has been said, 'You shall not tempt the LORD your God.'" Now when the devil had ended every temptation, he departed from Him until an opportune time. (Luke 4:1-13)

As we can see from the scripture, Satan begins his challenge to Jesus in asking questions of His identity;"… if you are the son of God…" This is a question asked to challenge Jesus' identity. It is like asking, "If you think you know yourself that well…?"

Alternatively, "who do you think you are?"

Anyone who wants to see him or her accomplishing his or her life's goals must answer the questions objectively and not based on fantasies or wishes.

When you have discovered who you really are, you will:

- Progress rapidly in life

- Gain more self-confidence and be assertive

- Be happier and at peace within yourself

- Be more socially sensitive

- To make the right choices for your life

- To live a more fulfilled life.

We would at this point employ an analytical tool to assist us in the discovery of who we are. This is the SWOT analysis; which I have borrowed from business management theory. It is an analytical framework used to determine the position of an organisation within an industry. In other words, they use the SWOT to find their current position and then decide which strategy to adopt, in order to increase their level of performance.

S – Strength: Discover Where Your Strength Lie

In identifying who you are, you need to discover what your strengths are. Where do your strengths lie? Every one of us has one thing or the other that not many people can match. Lynn Johnston remarked once that 'We are all born with wonderful gifts. We use these gifts to express ourselves, to amuse, to strengthen, and to communicate. We begin as children to explore and develop our talents, often unaware that we are unique, that not everyone can do what we're doing!'

The area of your strength lies in what you do without difficulty. This seems to come out of inherent interest. Is it in talking, writing, cooking, narrating events, role playing, convincing people, speaking into the lives of other people to bring about change? You need to discover what it may be.

Your Strength Distinguishes You From Others

Your strength can also be referred to as your core competencies. It is like your area of speciality. Unlike skills or knowledge, you can acquire strength through education; your strengths are talents that are more basic. For most parts, you were born with them. You may continuously develop new talents but about your strengths, you have unfair advantage. In fact, you cannot even teach someone to be as good as you are unless you have strength in that particular area.

When we take the story of Samson and Delilah for instance, Samson revealed that his strength was from the Spirit of God and hence the statement "... if you cut my hair the Spirit of God would leave me and become like any other ordinary man". In other words, what makes a person special and defines him or her is not so much, of what he or she has inherited but what they developed as their strength.

Look Within, For Your Strength

Available statistics show that your strength plays an important role in acquisition of wealth and not by inheritance as many of us might have thought. This does not undermine the fact that wealth can be acquired by inheritance. It is just to stress the point that you can create your own wealth without waiting on someone to die in order to inherit him or her.

According to a study of Federal Reserve (USA) data conducted by NYU professor Edward Wolff, for the nation's richest 1%, inherited wealth accounted for only 9% of their net worth in 2001, down from 23% in 1989. (The 2001 number was the latest available.)

According to a study by Prince & Associates, less than 10% of today's multi-millionaires cited "inheritance" as their source of wealth.

A study by Spectrem Group found that among today's millionaires, inherited wealth accounted for just 2% of their total sources of wealth.

Each of these stats measures slightly different things, yet they all come to the same basic conclusion: *Inheritance is not the main driver of today's wealth.* The reason we have had a doubling in the number of millionaires and billionaires over the past decade (even adjusted for inflation) is that more of the non-wealthy have become wealthy.

So it is not just that the same old rich folks are getting richer. The more-important shift is that the rich are getting more numerous.[38]

This is a clear indication that people are using their strengths to be successful with very few depending on what is passed on to them.

Discovering your strength is partly an answer to the identity question and positions you to win in your wilderness.

Most of the time, the strength a person possesses discloses what his assignment on earth is; Furthermore, what a person's assignment is leads to revealing who he is.

W – Weakness: Identify What Your Weaknesses Are

In as much as practice develops precision and precision is like the sharp edge of a knife. In the same way as every individual has strength so, do you have weaknesses? What are your weaknesses? If you could identify some of the things you struggle doing, you are close to identifying what your weaknesses are. There are instances where a person can develop an area of weakness in order to surmount it. People who were once told they could never read have overcome that weakness to read but to become prolific writers.

Most of the time at interviews, we are asked the question "what are your weaknesses? Frankly, most interviewers do not realistically expect an honest answer like "I don't get on well with team members". The recognition that one posses the weakness helps reveal that the applicant poses qualities such as sincerity, piquancy, self awareness and the skills necessary to manage shortcomings and mistakes. More importantly beyond interview, do we need to answer these queries in our private time to help us know which areas we may need to work on?

O – Opportunity: Sample Your Opportunity

You may have heard this saying "opportunity comes but once", is not entirely true. Opportunity comes to everyone in life. The opportunities you choose or opt for defines who you are. It is not every opportunity that is intended for your progress. The knowledge of your potential strength and weaknesses would help you to select from the opportunities you are bestowed. What you identify as an opportunity is informed by your strengths and weaknesses. Two sales personnel were sent by their company to another town to study the market to open a branch of their company's shoe shop. When they got there, they found out that the people in that town did not wear shoes. One of the sales personnel reported to their Headquarters that they could not open an outlet because the people did not wear shoes. The other also reported that the people did not wear shoes and as a result, they could create the need for shoes and sell them shoes. The sales personnel who saw the opportunity to sell shoes to these people without shoes believes he or she has the strength to sell the shoes. As a result, his strengths made him see the opportunity.

T – Threats: Compile A List Of Your Threats

These situations or circumstances shut you out from engaging yourself in activities that involves the use of your initiative and creativity. Anything that affects your ability to perform at your highest stratum is a threat to the discovery of who you are.

Anyone will protect what is important to him or her and what is important to him or her to a point defines who a person is.

Your identity will be questioned as Jesus' was questioned, as this was unavoidable in the wilderness of Jesus' life. The interesting issue is that this challenge came at a point when Jesus had forsaken all pleasures of food and social contact to be alone with God. If Jesus had no idea of who he was then he would have turned the stones into bread or bowed to Satan for the kingdoms of the world. Like Jesus, the prime mover and the finisher of our faith, if we discover who we are, we will win the battle in the middle.

Point Two: The Garden

Then Jesus came with them to a place called Gethsemane, and said to the disciples, "Sit here while I go and pray over there." And He took with Him Peter and the two sons of Zebedee, and He began to be sorrowful and deeply distressed. Then He said to them, "My soul is exceedingly sorrowful, even to death. Stay here and watch with Me." He went a little farther and fell on His face, and prayed, saying, "O My Father, if it is possible, let this cup pass from Me; nevertheless, not as I will, but as You will." Then He came to the disciples and found them sleeping, and said to Peter, "What! Could you not watch with Me one hour? Watch and pray, lest you enter into temptation. The spirit indeed is willing, but the flesh is weak."

Again, a second time, He went away and prayed, saying, "O My Father, if this cup cannot pass away from Me unless I drink it, Your will be done." And He came and found them asleep again, for their eyes were heavy.

So He left them, went away again, and prayed the third time, saying the same words. Then He came to His disciples and said to them, "Are you still sleeping and resting? Behold, the hour is at hand, and the Son of Man is being betrayed into the hands of sinners. Rise, let us be going. See, My betrayer is at hand."(Matthew 26:36-46)

Coming out, He went to the Mount of Olives, as He was accustomed, and His disciples also followed Him. When He came to the place, He said to them, "Pray that you may not enter into temptation." And He was withdrawn from them about a stone's throw, and He knelt down and prayed, saying, "Father, if it is Your will, take this cup away from Me; nevertheless not My will, but Yours, be done." Then an angel appeared to Him from heaven, strengthening Him. And being in agony, He prayed more earnestly. Then His sweat became like great drops of blood falling down to the ground.

When He rose up from prayer, and had come to His disciples, He found them sleeping from sorrow. Then He *said to them, "Why do you sleep? Rise and pray, lest you enter into temptation." (Luke 22:39-46)*

Gethsemane was an area geographically located at the foot of the Mount of Olives. It is therefore no coincidence at all that the meaning of Gethsemane is oil press. The implication is that the olives obtained from the groves were pressed for oil probably at this location. What could have moved Jesus to the extent that the sweat from His body was like drops of blood? He had a burden about the death that was awaiting Him to an extent that angels came down to strengthen Him. You can have an ugly problem in a serene and beautiful place. You may be reading this material at this time in a beautiful home or car, and yet you have an ugly problem. You have a habit you are struggling with, a secret you cannot afford to make known at any time. Many admire you and your position in life yet you know there is much than meets the eye in your life. Whatever horrid problems you have, I pray, God reaches out to you in the same way angels ministered to our Lord Jesus Christ. There is no situation too difficult that God cannot handle. His eyes are on the sparrows, and He watches over you too.

For the things that you must necessarily go through, receive the divine strength to go through and overcome them. No matter how ugly your problem may be, whether it is a debt, barrenness, terminal illness, divorce, death of a loved one just to name a few, He will come through for you. Remember what He states in Psalm 66:12b "we went through fire and through water, but you brought us out to rich fulfillment". You will come out in a much better state than you were before all the troubles began. You are not alone. The Lord is with you.

There are four incidents in the context of the story from Matthew 26 from which we can learn.

The garden is a place of:

Pressure

Prayer

Perspiration

Preparation

We shall have an in depth discussion of each of the above and how they apply to our lives.

A Place Of Pressure: No One Can Feel It The Way You Do

The Webster's dictionary presents us with two definitions of pressure:

- The force produced by pressing.

- The force of an urgent claim or demand

The garden was by no means a place of tranquillity the instant Jesus stepped in there. He was extremely sorrowful and was at the place where he might pour his burdens onto his father. Jesus was feeling the force of an urgent claim or demand on his life, first, the fact that he will no longer be seeing and having physical companionship with his friends, family, and disciples among others. He went into the garden with his disciples that they may provide him with some form of support, but they slept. Do you sometimes feel lonely because no one can truly share your burdens? They tell you they are with you, and yet they cannot feel what you can feel. It is even more irksome when you phone up prayer partners and tell them of your problems and sometimes their prayer seems empty without the passion you had expected. They cannot feel what you feel and most of the times have no idea of your pain. This is exactly the experience of Jesus in Gethsemane. He asked his disciples when he found them sleeping "could you not watch with me for an hour?" they slept on Christ when they were supposed to be there providing him with prayer support.

Good People Experience Pressure Too

Jesus knew exactly the enormity of the suffering that was awaiting him. This was the reason he could ask the father: "let this cup pass me by" (Matthew 26:39). He knew how his family, friends and disciples revered him. To think about being paraded through the city naked was unbearable as it would have been for you and me. Think about all the people he healed, cast out devils from, those he rebuked, sympathizers, and foes alike in the crowd watching him being beaten, spat upon and put to death. This man went about doing good and now being scoffed at like an evil doer, a real case of falsehood triumphing over truth. How difficult this would have been for Jesus? Whatever he had to go through, he chose that above his snugness, he chose to go through the pain and died for you. He chose you, he thought of you above all. Reminisce it was not an easy choice for him to make, and yet he made that choice although he knew it was going to cost him his life. In the midst of the pending pressure of ignominy, pain, humiliation and death, he had the joy to see you free from the shackles of Satan.

You Always Have A Lot More To Give Than You Think

In negligible terms juxtaposing to what Jesus felt, you recall how it feels like when you have given your all and yet more is required. This could happen in the job at your workplace or on your course work at school. You may be reading this book and you are faced with the collapse of your business that is your main source of income although you are giving it 110% of your efforts. You may be a single parent finding it extremely and increasingly difficult combining full time work and caring for your children. It feels like being given the task of mixing water with oil, very stressful and difficult to mix. As Jesus did in his situation, be motivated by the result of your struggles. Fix your eyes on the price and get through with it. You may find yourself in a tight place and under pressure at present, but that is the worst experience that you can ever have. Something beneficial, rewarding and valuable should be birthed out of all these.

You Can Identify With the Olive Fruit

We have already described the fact that Gethsemane was geographically located at the base of the olive grove and for that, matter is no coincidence, why Gethsemane means oil press. We appreciate the use of the olive oil, either for cooking or in anointing people with prayer among its many uses. We will therefore not appreciate the process through which the oil is pressed out from the olive fruit. On the garbage dump, somewhere may be lying a discoloured, crashed and a traumatized piece of an olive fruit from which the oil was extracted. It is only when an olive fruit is pressed that oil can be extracted. However, the process is not a thrilling one for the olive. There are times that for God to bring out the best in us, He allows us to go through moments and situations of great pressure. Do not be weary;

you are yet to see the best come out of you.

Pressure Uncovers The Gems We Are

Every pressure applied must produce something positive out of your life to bless someone. We earlier on defined pressure, as the force produced by pressing, the pressing of the olive may not be convenient but by force, something is produced. Force in itself is defined as strength or energy and this energy can be used positively. Whenever you are under pressure, remember something better is going to happen when all is over. Let us look at the life of world icons such as Nelson Mandela and Martin Luther King Jr.,

Nelson Mandela for instance became even more popular with concerts being organised to petition his release from prison. More pressure groups that are non-political were formed to pressurize the South African government for his release. For 27 years, he was incarcerated under the apartheid, system, but he only came out to fight for independence of South Africa in 1994 and went on to become its first black president. He had become a respected statesman and an icon of mature leadership. He now has a statue of himself in Parliament Square in London. He has taught that bitterness is a choice out of several options on hand in times of ill treatments and pain imposed by an oppressor. People celebrate him for this reason. You too can become better and not bitter.

Pressure Also Comes Even When Fighting For Others

Martin Luther King Jr in leading the black civil rights movement fighting against obnoxious segregation laws in the south of the United States. He had to endure many times of needless incarcerations, police dogs attacks, and swept off his feet with high-pressure water from hoses. Eventually he was shot and died at a prime age. These pressures and the unwillingness of the government of those states to repeal those laws made him well known and one of the most respected leaders of American Civil Rights history. These pressures gave him the opportunities to appeal before kings and princes around the world. This includes an opportunity to address the house of congress of the United States and a special guest of the independence celebration at the invitation of Ghana's first president, Dr Kwame Nkrumah. He is the youngest person ever to receive the Nobel Peace Prize.

For most times inventions are birthed in times of necessity. After all what is tea without hot water poured. Fix your eyes on the things about to happen in your life due to the pressure and not the pain of the pressure itself. Choose to be better when all is said and done instead of being bitter. Disallow any individual who wants to choose for you your responses to any situation of difficulty and pain. Be in control of your actions and reactions choose them rationally.

A Place Of Prayer: Not Only When We Are Overwhelmed

It is awe-inspiring how our Lord Jesus Christ went to a place of solitude to meet with the Father when he was exceedingly sorrowful. For some of us, our first point of call in time of need and trouble is a friend or family who in some cases cannot help much. It was obvious no amount of encouragement and comfort would have relieved Jesus of his burden.

One other issue we need to consider is the fact that this was not the only time Jesus went into prayer. We find in Mark 6:46 'And when He sent them away, He departed to the mountain to pray', that Jesus has a custom of praying always is why He could admonish the disciples to pray and not faint (see Mark 14:38). Prayer should be the lifestyle of the believer. We do not only pray because we are in dire need of something but, because prayer is the core to the building up of a believer's life. As we have already examined in an earlier chapter.

The foundation to the life we are building has already been laid, but the construction of the super structure involves prayer. Well, one of the materials is prayer – praying in the Holy Spirit (see Jude 20, 21).

In the context of the scripture, we are examining. Jesus went to the garden to pour out his burdens because it was too much to bear. For this reason, the father sent angels to minister to Him. Develop a lifestyle of seeking the face of God, a time when you can offload your burdens to Him. He is willing to carry them for you.

'casting all your care upon Him, for He cares for you' (1 Peter 5:7)

The weight o a person's burden determines the depth of a person's prayer. Apart from the garden being a place of off loading Jesus' burdens, it was also a place of the battle of wills.

Align Your Will To The Will Of God

It was in the garden of Gethsemane that Jesus surrendered His will to God about going to the cross. It was clear that if Jesus had options He might have sought for another way out when death was staring Him in the face. In spite of His apprehensions, He placed the will of God for coming to the earth above His. It is in prayer that we submit our will to the will of God. This is because God gave man dominion over the earth as found in Genesis 1:26 therefore, for God to do anything here on earth, He has to wait until there is an alignment of the will of men to what He intends to do. God created us, as beings with a will and the freedom to make choices not imposing His will on us. We therefore need to submit our will to Him if we intend to have the life we really want.

Position Yourself To Know God's Next Move

Then the LORD appeared to him by the terebinth trees of Mamre, as he was sitting in the tent door in the heat of the day.2 So he lifted his eyes and looked, and behold, three men were standing by him; and when he saw them, he ran from the tent door to meet them, and bowed himself to the ground, and said, "My Lord, if I have now found favor in Your sight, do not pass on by Your servant. Please let a little water be brought, and wash your feet, and rest yourselves under the tree. And I will bring a morsel of bread, that you may refresh your hearts. After that you may pass by, inasmuch as you have come to your servant." They said, "Do as you have said."

So Abraham hurried into the tent to Sarah and said, "Quickly, make ready three measures of fine meal; knead it and make cakes." And Abraham ran to the herd, took a tender and good calf, gave it to a young man, and he hastened to prepare it. (Genesis 18:1-7)

Then the men rose from there and looked toward Sodom,

and Abraham went with them to send them on the way. And the LORD said, "Shall I hide from Abraham what I am doing, since Abraham shall surely become a great and mighty nation, and all the nations of the earth shall be blessed in him? (Genesis 18:16-18)

God would send angels to Sodom and Gomorrah to destroy the city and yet gave Abraham the chance to negotiate to spare a few righteous men and women living there. This goes to buttress the point why the scriptures say in Amos 3:7 '... He does nothing without revealing it to his servants the prophets...' The answer to the many questions about the many sufferings of people through famine, many other natural disasters is this; we have not yet submitted to Him our lives, and our nations, though He is willing to help us. In some cases where we say we have, we still tend to do it our own way. Often the result is below the measured performance of God or of what can be attributed to Him.

Know How To Determine The Will Of God

He made known His ways to Moses, His acts to the children of Israel. (Psalm 103:7)

Many people struggle with determining what the will of God is in order to be able to align their will to the will of God. Sometimes we think the will of God is what we want to do that God does not want us to do.

One of the things I have to point out is that we submit to the will of God in freedom. He does not force us to do anything against our will. Moses proved that if one knows the ways of God it makes it less complicated to identify what the will of God is. This supports my statement that most people struggle with finding the will of God in any given situation.

You Can Determine The Will Of God By Revelation

We read in many places where Moses is summoned onto the mountain to meet in person with God. The intimate fellowship, which Moses shared with God, gave him the opportunity to know Him better and thus His will.

Through the word of God

Moses wrote the first five books of the Old Testament referred to as Pentateuch, so where did Moses learn about God? Some scholars maintain some of Moses writings wcrc passed on by oral tradition. This does not however change the fact of the bible was written under the inspiration of the Spirit of God. However, for us, we have the entire bible to help us and to guide us since it is the Word of God.

Through A Matured Believer - 'Jethro the priest of Median'

So when Moses' father-in-law saw all that he did for the people, he said, "What is this thing that you are doing for the people? Why do you alone sit, and all the people stand before you from morning until evening?" (Exodus 18:14)

At the point when Moses was carrying out his responsibilities, Jethro a priest who had also walked with God offered him advice. The advice is what has come to be known as the principle of delegation. There are times when mature believers can provide godly advice and direction based on their experience with God.

Judge His Ways Correctly

God deals with everyone differently. God cannot be prognosticated as far as His ways are concerned. Whatever He says He does above what we can ask or even think (Isaiah 55:8).

God does not operate by our standard time. He lives in a timeless realm. Psalm 90:4. He is immortal and eternal.

God is not the author of confusion, but uses problems as the midwife to birth His purposes in the life of His people. He chooses the foolish things of this world to confound the wise.

Complete Your Job In Prayer Before You Physically Start

but with the precious blood of Christ, as of a lamb without blemish and without spot. 20 He indeed was foreordained before the foundation of the world, but was manifest in these last times for you (1 Peter 1:19-20)

God has a character of finishing things before He starts out altogether. Jesus was ordained a sacrifice for humankind even before the earth and the world were formed. Again, in Jeremiah 1:4-5 God reveals to Jeremiah, He had made adequate plans for him, even before he was conceived. Jesus finished the work of the cross in terms of the pain and suffering, He was to go through in the garden in prayer. Like Jesus, we need to seek the face of God and have circumstances totally worked out in the Spirit before we even set out to accomplish it. Most of us will start some of life's endeavours and in the first instance inform friends, even before we commit them to God. As it was His custom, He began each day with prayer in solitude. The middle is about the release of God's power to take over our human frailties and to enable us accomplish God's purposes for our lives.

A Place Of Perspiration: Birth What You Carry On The inside

'And being in agony, He prayed more earnestly. Then His sweat became like great drops of blood falling down to the ground' (Luke 22:44)

Perspiration is another word for sweat. Sweat is a salty liquid given off by the body through the pulse of the skin and helps the body to stay in cool. It is interesting to know God sent angels to strengthen Jesus. Grace is released when we spend time perspiring in the presence of God. It is normal that you sweat most of the time when you use energy. Thomas A. Edison has said that 'Genius is one percent inspiration, ninety-nine percent perspiration'.

Push A Little Bit More

That notwithstanding, sometimes life's problems catch up us when we are weak and do not have enough strength to fight anymore. We say 'if only this problem had come ten, fifteen or twenty years earlier, I would have been able to face it squarely and handle it well. However, now I'm tired and can't stand it anymore.' It is at that time that you rather push because as you do, angels will be on stand by to help you out. As we might have seen the middle would make mental, psychological and physical demands on you, and you should be able to meet demands if you want to stay through to the end. It is written in Proverbs 24:10 'If you faint in the day of adversity, Your strength is small', but we would not fail in the face of adversity because even when our strength is gone, He makes us strong as it was in the case of Jesus.

A Place Of Preparation: Good Preparation Means Good Performance

In life, before there is a performance or accomplishment, there is preparation because:

- Life is not designed for the weak.

- Life is not designed for the faint hearted

- Life is not for those who have made provision to chicken out.

- Life is not designed for people who have enough tears to shed for every problem.

The word preparation is defined as something done in readiness for something else. The reason Jesus could go through His middle was preparation. Jesus had to be mentally tough to endure such pain and suffering. Jesus would have quit if He were not mentally tough after some maltreatment was meted out to Him. Most of the time, mental toughness is associated with athletes but has a general application for most areas of our lives. Mental toughness is having the natural or developed psychological edge that enables you to cope better than others do with many demands[39].

There are key psychological characteristics associated with mentally tough elite athletes, you can learn. This is based on a research conducted by the University of Pennsylvania on successful athletes.

Key One: You must have self-belief; they had an unshakable belief in their ability to achieve competition goals.

Key Two: You must be motivated; they had an insatiable desire, an internalized motivation to succeed and they could bounce back from performance set back with increased determination to succeed.

Key Three: You must be focussed; they remained focused on the task.

Key Four: You must be composed; they can regain psychological control following unexpected events or distractions.

You May Have Too Much Than You Can Handle, It May Seem

Life does not always present us with situations that are easier to handle, there are situations that are very difficult to handle and yet to get to the next stage of our lives, we need to deal with them. It is difficult to say to you that in order for you to develop mental toughness you need practice. This may not be what you wanted to read but the fact remains that it is through practice and training that an athlete develop endurance to the pain of their sport. It is when they have been through that repeatedly that pain is no longer a bother.

Point Three: The Cross

And when Jesus had cried out with a loud voice, He said, "Father, 'into Your hands I commit My spirit.' Having said this, He breathed His last. (Luke 23:46)

As part of the process of Jesus accomplishing His purpose here on earth, He had a middle to manage. The cross was one gruesome episode, which will make one shudder. Apart from the pain and death, the cross was considered a punishment and a curse. Do you know how it feels to be falsely portrayed to the public? He was a man who had done no wrong and yet made a by-word and ridicule. The comfort we get out of all this is that our Lord and master has been through it and can help us through it too.

The experience of the crucifixion presented Jesus Christ once again with three moments as part of the process of the middle.

A moment of loneliness feeling

A moment you will be misunderstood

A moment of yielding your spirit (the core of your being).

Moment One: You Will Have a Moment of Loneliness Feeling

For a brief moment in Jesus' life, He felt lonely. He felt as though he was detached from the Father. This was a man who is one with the father (see John 10:30), crying out as if He has been left on his own to go through all by Himself. Some bible scholars believe that at that moment, the entire sin of the world had been placed upon Him and because God hates sin, He could not anymore stand His only begotten son.

The feeling Jesus had was not a feeling of solitude because there were people all around him. The disciples were there, the roman soldiers; although hostile had a presence there, His mother, siblings and other sympathizing women were all present.

And a great multitude of the people followed Him, and women who also mourned and lamented Him. But Jesus, turning to them, said, "Daughters of Jerusalem, do not weep for Me, but weep for yourselves and for your children. (Luke 23:27-28)

Your Loneliness Is Not Externally Imposed

Loneliness is not about what goes on around you, on the outside it is what goes on within you. You can be married with or without children and be lonely to an extent that someone who is single would not have this experience. You could even belong to a big church, go to a highly populated school and still be lonely because it is simply a feeling of detachment. This feeling sometimes for us goes beyond the physical where we feel God has forsaken us. This happens when we feel heaven is quiet on us and the only response we hear in reply to our calls is the echo of our cry for help.

When it comes to silence of heaven on us, you need to understand that this could be one of two things. Firstly, you may be farther away from God. A man went to the forest with his youngest son to hunt. He then asked his son to take another direction to look for his game too, not far from where he was. To determine how farther apart they were, the father told the son that every ten minutes, he would call out his name and the fainter he could hear his voice, he should know they were drifting too far apart. The lesson here is that there are times we drift too far away from the Father that even when He speaks, we can hardly hear. It is time to develop some intimacy with the father, spend quality time in his presence, studying the word of God, praying and worshiping.

Secondly, there may be silence from heaven as part of our training of trusting God one-step at a time to accomplish what he has said he will do. In Luke, 2:51 that was the last time anything was heard about Jesus until he resurfaced again at age thirty ready to fulfil his God given mandate. The silent years as some have referred to is the time for developing all the virtues needed for the accomplishment of that purpose you carry. In addition, at the fullness of time, you shall be manifested to the world, but until then keep trusting God and building yourself up in your faith in God.

Misconceptions about Loneliness

When people feel lonely sometimes, they think:

- Loneliness is a sign of weakness or immaturity.

- There is something wrong with them.

- They are the only ones that feel the way they feel.

As long as you continue to hold on to these misconceptions, then you will develop complexes and have the conditions described below:

Condition One: Inferiority complex

This is evaluating yourself against others in negative terms and so expects people to reject you. What you need to understand is that, you have your own shortcomings, but you are not alone. Everyone on this planet have a weakness or shortcoming. Focus on what your strengths is, making an effort to improve in the areas of your life where you are weak. For God send His only son to die for you shows how important and precious you are in the sight of God. It is in this light you need to see yourself. Focus on what you have and can do and not on what others make you think you do not have.

Condition Two: Lack of Assertiveness

There are people who have failed an interview because they were not assertive. Assertiveness is not having pride; instead, it is an attitude and a way of relating to the outside world, backed up by a set of skills for effective communication. This stems from seeing yourself as being of worth, whilst acknowledging the same about others. Loneliness is possible to make you less assertive, less responsive and likely to approach social encounters with cynicism and mistrust. You are not sure who loves you, who do not, and so you keep to yourself. During Jesus' trial (Luke 23:3), He was not shy to reveal who He was when asked by

Pilate to confirm His identity. Be less bothered about what people think about you, what you think about yourself is what is important.

What Do You Do If You Feel Lonely?

Work at developing your social skills

Practice getting to know others and letting them know you. You can only make friends when you first make yourself friendly (see Proverbs 18:24). As you try to make friends, avoid judging the people you come across due to past relationships. This is quite relevant when you have been hurt in a previous relationship. You tend to be extra cautious in your dealings with people.

Think of your loneliness as an opportunity to develop independence and learn to take care of your own emotional needs.

There are people who are into marriage in order that they may get benefit from the companionship not to be good company to their partners. This could be disappointing as you become overbearing on your companion or partner.

Exercise Regularly

Many self-help books on health prescribe as a remedy for many diseases among others, good nutrition, regular exercises and adequate rest. What you need to understand is that, loneliness is an emotional problem therefore being in the right frame of mind is a result of a right functioning body. Do you realize that when you exercise in the morning before going to work, you have an amazing mental alertness?

Moment Two: A Moment of Being Misunderstood

As you strive to stand out of the billions of humans on earth as yourself, you should expect people to misunderstand you. You have to understand that you carry destiny and that others cannot figure out what you are. In the middle, as you seek to build your life this is a moment to expect. If it has not happened it will happen, it is a sign that you stand out.

As a remedy to being misunderstood, misquoted, misrepresented and misjudged, there are two things to watch out for Skill and Precision.

Develop Proficiency

This is a special ability or proficiency. David can be considered to have a skill in stone slinging. Before David faced Goliath, he picked five stones and yet used just one. When Saul tried to give him armour, he rejected it, simply because it was not his area of expertise or his special ability. The use of your skill would be the means to silence your critics because you would not have many explanations to do. David's brothers mistook his coming to the battlefield as coming to see the battle. What else would they have to say on his conquest of Goliath? They should be proud of him. His brothers were now going to know the difference between what they perceived to be his motives and what actually happened.

Develop Precision

This means exact, accurate in every detail. Still taking David's story, the stone he threw landed on the exact spot as he has intended. Goliath had armour on and according to some bible commentators, the visor that covered Goliath face might have moved upwards exposing some parts of his face, exactly the place David's stone struck. Precision is to a skill as a sharp edge is to a knife. Think about it, those who cannot stand your success and personal development would be silenced. Skill with precision would make you excellent.

Moment Three: A Moment of Yielding Your Spirit

God made men out of the dust of the ground, breathed into him the breath of life (His Spirit) and then men became a living soul (will, emotion, intellect). In the context of the scripture, Jesus yielding up His spirit meant dying, actually other translations as the King James Versions puts it as "gave up the ghost". The spirit of humans is the very core of man's being. It is what makes you what you are. It is the real you. Other verses of scripture refer to the spirit of man as the inner man (see Ephesians3:16). By extension, the yielding of your spirit is yielding the core of your being, it is yielding anything that makes you who you are; your personality, respect, achievements and dignity among many others to God. To get through your middle, you need to yield your life in its entirety to God.

I also might have confidence in the flesh. If anyone else thinks he may have confidence in the flesh, I more so: circumcised the eighth day, of the stock of Israel, of the tribe of Benjamin, a Hebrew of the Hebrews; concerning the law, a Pharisee; concerning zeal, persecuting the church; concerning the righteousness which is in the law, blameless. But what things were gain to me, these I have counted loss for Christ. (Philippians 3:4-7)

Paul describes the many credentials he brings to the table of human rankings:

Credential One: Circumcised On The Eighth Day

That is to say that I am a descendant of Abraham, which is the pride of all Jewish and Arabic people.

Credential Two: Concerning The Law A Pharisee

Paul was considered a learned and highly educated individual. For some bible commentators, it was the reason why he could plant many churches about two-thirds of the New Testament churches.

Credential Three: Concerning Zeal, Second To None

He again had totally sold himself out for the work of God. For him the kingdom, its stability, expansion and influence preoccupied him above all.

Credential Four: Concerning Righteousness Of The Law, Blameless

He expressed his loyalty to the rule of God upon his life.

You Are Guaranteed A Place At The Top

Paul considered all these as a profit and an advantage to him and yet thought about them as nothing. The things that gave him a higher ranking in the sight of men, he has given up, so that he may gain Christ. Let us be like Jesus who made himself of no reputation and even submitted himself to a disgraceful death though He had an option to die or otherwise (Philippians 2:5-9) yet it is for this same reason that God has exalted Him. You would by no means loose anything, yielding your all unto God. He will exalt you beyond heights your strength would permit you.

You are guaranteed a place at the top, if you would yield all to Him. Jesus has shown us the way; would you yield your entire being to Him now? He would not reject you. He exalts those who humble themselves under His authority. If you can do this now, you are destined for the top.

Help I am in the middle!

The most difficult situation for any individual, proprietor, CEO, manager, Pastor, Teacher, Builder etc to be in, is to know there is the potential to accomplish any task and yet cannot pull it off due to obstacles. There are always two options in these situations, you either choose to give it up or choose to hold on and continue in your quest for a way to go through it. We have already said that God has a character of finishing off things, even before He starts its physical manifestation. As a result, when God speaks to us about our future of what He is going to do, He has already finished that as part of His blue print for us. It is the reason we could say, 'let the weak say I'm strong and the poor say I'm rich', even before we experienced it. We have been made strong and rich only discovering how strong and rich we are. It is true that in most of our present circumstances is not a true picture of who we are.

God is the one who has established our future and have revealed it to us without revealing to us what we need to go through. For everyone who has a vision, a dream, an ambition, a future and a life to build, the middle is not avoidable. Unfortunately, many people like you, have the joy of the visions cut short, the conceptions of their dreams aborted because they could not master the middle.

We Can Learn From Abraham And Sarah's Story

Abraham is referred to as the father of faith because he knew how to handle the middle that he was confronted with. He was given a promise by God but between the promise and the fulfillment was about a twenty-five year waiting period to deal with; that is the middle.

Lesson One: Physical Possibilities May Be Fading Away But Hold On

They had to deal with the pressure of seeing they grow older with the possibilities of having children fading away completely with each passing day. Their bodies were getting weaker and weaker as each day, month and year passed by. Do we sometimes experience this in our own lives when we think our finite mortality is catching up with us without any sign of the promises showing up? This could be about you, who have received great promises about your calling and ministry, and yet you seem not be having that break. You may not be in ministry but in business or single person with promises, the hope of which seems to be fading away with the passing of time.

Lesson Two: Friends May Ridicule You But Hold On

They might have had to deal with the ridicule from friends and neighbours about having many, ripe ready and fertile maidservants and still without a child. You might be facing some ridicule due to a lack in your life or the presence of some unfortunate circumstance, but you need to be strong and hold on as Abraham did.

Lesson Three: You May Feel Deceived But Hold On

He had to deal with the deception that maybe God has forgotten about them or maybe God cannot even do what He says He will do. He succeeded to parry all those thoughts out of his mind, to prevent it from making a serious impression on him and thereby taking an action.

Do not entertain thoughts of doubt on what God can do. He can keep His promises. He does not fail, you need to have patience and wait for Him.

Lesson Four: You Must Increase Your Ability to wait

Patience is as the ability to sit back and wait for an expected outcome without experiencing anxiety, tension or frustration. It also has to do with letting go of your need for immediate gratification. That which God has promised would come to pass but most of the time you need to wait. Abraham and Sarah had to wait for close to 25 years for the promised son, Isaac. Your ability to wait is based on your level of patience, and therefore you need to increase the level of your patience. Below are few suggestions though not exhaustive, which can be of help.

Lesson Five: You Must Develop A Consistent Philosophy of Life.

Take life one day at a time. Consider each day as a gift of life that will allow you to get one-step closer to your life's goals. Learn to take one-step at a time: "a little at a time always at it".

Accept the reality of your humanity in that you are going to need time, effort and energy to work out your dreams, visions, aspirations and your life as a whole. As you increase in knowledge of the world around you, understanding the purposes and plan of God, you tend to become more aware that you are only human. This is something that Sarah knew very well; when she laughed at the angels of God who said she was going have a child a year on. For that matter, there are things you may not be able to do promptly. Remember the world was not all created in a day. Beautiful symphonies, works of art and literary masterpieces were not created in a day. A lifetime is not lived in a day.

Lesson Six: Modify your Spiritual Perspective to Include God

Jesus was successful dealing with the middle in His life, and we can ask Him to help you deal with yours. He is more than willing to help you, if you are willing. The middle is very scary and frustrating, but we need not fear, God will not bring you this far to disgrace you. He does not disappoint those who put their trust in Him. You shall definitely get through with your assignment. Cheer up it is only the middle.

PART

FOUR

Even When The Building Seems To Be Finished

Another flaw in the human character is that everybody wants to build and nobody wants to do maintenance.

- Kurt Vonnegut

6

MAINTAINING WHAT YOU BUILD TO SUSTAIN YOUR ACCOMMPLSHMENTS

The intelligent man is one who has successfully fulfilled many accomplishments, and is yet willing to learn more. **- Ed Parker**

The joy of every accomplishment in life is being able to maintain it for posterity. When you have passed through the middle with all the difficulties and struggles and got some things done in your life, you should be able to maintain them. Many people do not have good maintenance culture, and so we strive hard to build some things in life, only to neglect them after sometime to decay. We need to emulate God in the way He thinks. His promise to Abraham (see Gen. 12:1-3), was that he will bless him and make him a blessing. God thinks in trans-generational terms, beyond the present.

Be Considered A Good Person

A good man leaves an inheritance to his children's children, But the wealth of the sinner is stored up for the righteous. (Proverbs 13: 22)

The goodness of the man is not based on the wealth he has but the fact that he preserves it for his descendants. For whatever we strive to build in our lifetime with the help of God, is just not meant for us, but those who are yet to be born. People who are yet to be born are going to depend on whatever God is using you for or helping you to build in life now. Do not let them down please!

We also have to understand as well that, what we have been able to build, whether our life, vision is etc.., is no longer yours you are only stewards. What does it mean to be a steward?

And above all things have fervent love for one another, for "love will cover a multitude of sins." Be hospitable to one another without grumbling. As each one has received a gift, minister it to one another, as good stewards of the manifold grace of God. If anyone speaks, let him speak as the oracles of God. If anyone ministers, let him do it as with the ability which God supplies, that in all things God may be glorified through Jesus Christ, to whom belong the glory and the dominion forever and ever. Amen. (1 Peter 4:8-11)

The word steward is defined "as a manager or superintendent of another's household". This is exactly what God has made each one of us, the things we have are things He has given to us in order for us to manage for Him. In other words, whatever you have been given is not yours you are only a manager. It is therefore right to say that there are people who are depending on you to become all they must become and vice versa. In Reference to the scripture quotation, it is not polemical whatsoever that everyone has a gift given by God, which is not limited to the example given in the text. The gifts given to every one are Love, Time and Life and there are those that are given to specific people like singing, advocating for people, encouraging the downhearted among others. The latter is given as a special ability beyond what people may naturally possess. For example, we can all sing but some are gifted to sing more harmoniously.

You Have Received The Gift of Love

We all have love in our hearts; there are people in our lives we love so dearly no matter the state or condition, they may be in. There are times our rows with friends, relatives and loved ones emanates from our deep love for them. There are times it is a misunderstanding, because you want them to understand your point of view and probably respond to issues the way we would have. We see these issues depicted daily, on our televisions, during daytime talk shows, where a dad would want his daughter to stay away from a drug-peddling boyfriend out of love and due to non-compliance from the daughter, there are always arguments at home. This sometimes develops to a stage where the girl leaves home entirely. This girl leaves home due to constant arguments but the arguments are because of the dad wanting to see the daughter back out of the relationship.

Most conflicts arise due to the disparity between expectation and reality. From a biblical perspective, true love is the God kind of love, which He has entrusted to us as stewards. It is even more demanding of believers to love even when others do not deserve to be loved. He has poured love into our hearts and this love must work for the benefit of others. Love poured into our hearts is intended to affect every area of our lives.

Find below how you can identify love at work in your life from 1 Corinthians 13:4-8 (see notes).

Characteristic One: Love is Patient

To be patient means bearing pains without complaining. There is this Bishop when it was time to leave his diocese gave a present to one of his laities who he felt had been a thorn in his flesh during his time at the parish. The other parishioners were extremely surprised because they knew this young woman did not seem to like the bishop that much. The bishop then explained that the woman's attitude taught him patience, and it was for that reason he was giving out the present.

Characteristic Two: Love is Kind

Love goes the extra mile and meets a need without expecting a reward. We live in a world where people look at you with scepticism when you go the extra mile to do something for them. They always tend to ask, "What's the catch"? This notwithstanding the fact that people are suspicious of receiving kindness, there are many great men and women who are working in war-ravaged countries helping people whose lives are torn apart by war. They go out of their way to show a little bit kindness to the many who are suffering as a result of senseless wars. Their kindness is the answer to the question of; what do they stand to gain from risking their lives for these victims? It can only be love in their hearts towards these victims that drive them to perform these acts of kindness.

Characteristic Three: Love is not Envious

Envy is the resentful awareness of an advantage enjoyed by another together with a desire to possess the same advantage. If we truly are children of God then we should not be envious of what others have achieved because it is to our complimentary advantage of also. Envy causes people to pull others down, use them as stepping-stones to the top. This is the reason why in some communities and households there are few champions and outstanding individuals. Everyone wants to be equal with the other person; there is a subtle competition, where people think supporting someone means handing them an undue advantage. Therefore there is a resentment to someone succeeding because in the minds of envious people, others succeeding is a statement of their own failures and inability to be as the succeeding individual. Where there is true love potentials are developed, assisted to be fulfilled and success by another is celebrated. Get rid of envy now. Call the people you envy now and tell them how great they are and congratulate them on their success.

Characteristic Four: Love is Not Boastful

Love does not draw needless attention to itself. There are people who are always talking about themselves and their family, business, dog, cat and their achievements. They are full of themselves. Some find it arduous to openly compliment and appreciate others for their achievement. If you cannot appreciate and compliment others, you may not receive a compliment either. Bear in mind you reap what you sow, you receive what you give. Learn to be appreciative of people. Keep your achievements to yourself until someone asks about them. Sometimes others who have not achieved what you have achieved may feel intimidated in your presence, if you are not saying it in an inspiring way. Your audience may consider what you say as a way of belittling their achievements also. If it is possible, give others the opportunity to share their own experiences too. Instead of telling them what you have achieved, ask them to tell you what they have done in the past or are in the process of doing tat has brought them a sense of pride and contentment.

Characteristic Five: Love is Not Selfish

When a person says they have love and yet cannot share with others what they have, and take everything for themselves without the consideration of others, the person is being selfish. Where there is true love people do not seek their own, in the story of Lot in Genesis 13:11, Lot decided to make a choice of the available land when his uncle should have given him a portion because God had given it to him. The land that he considered as best for him was not as he envisaged. In the end, he lost his wife and possessions when God rained fire on the land: Sodom and Gomorrah. Lot should have given the advantage to Abraham to choose first out of respect, since he had those possessions because of his association with Abraham. Rather he sought to outwit Abraham for the best portion of the land and unfortunately what he chose brought him misery and pain. Give people an equal opportunity you would give yourself. Do not provide them with half chances with the intention of having an advantage over them. This is selfishness and it is not a show of love.

Characteristic Six: Love is Not Easily Provoked

Provocation results from resentment. There are times issues may provoke a person to anger based on a past experience and may not necessarily related to current events. However, the current event triggers the provocation. God is looking for people who love and are not easily angered, not cantankerous and not quick-tempered. To be able to avoid being provoked give people the benefit of the doubt. Do not read too much meaning into people's actions to misconstrue their intentions. Ask them to clarify, if you are not sure about what their words or actions mean. This should help you to put into proper perspective your interpretations of people's words and actions. This would minimise provocation.

Characteristic Seven: Love Does Not Keep Records of Wrongs

There will always be the occasion to be offended by others. When a disciple asked Jesus 'how many times he needs to forgive people when they offend him', He responded seventy times seven (70x70). The principle is that by the time, you get to this point, you will be used to being offended without getting angry. We are not to keep records of people who offend us, whether in our minds or hearts. Anytime anyone offends you is the right time to forgive the individual and move on. This is the expression of love God wants us to exhibit.

Elements That Undermine The Practice Of Love

Element One: When You Esteem Yourself Highly Than Others

Jesus is an ultimate example when it comes to love. Even though He was equal with God, he did not boast about it; he chose to make himself of no reputation. He humbled himself even to the point of death. Love is undermined when one person sees himself or herself above the other, portraying the relationship between a suzerain and a subject. The subject respects and obeys the command of the suzerain because they have to and not due to love. We cannot say we love and yet despise or look down on people. There are times when you think others do not have good intentions towards you; you realize that your attitude towards them changes almost immediately. You may have smiles on your face when you see them and yet in your heart you resent them. We all have our opinions about things and issues and sometimes want to voice them out, but we need not be critical of others, whilst we may have the same problem. Be wary of a person who is too critical of others. This leads to reading meanings into people's actions, statements, and misinterpreting the actions and words of people.

Element Two: When You Do Not Make the Effort to Love

This is the main distinction between God and man. The Bible says 'let us love because God is love'. God does not make any effort to love, but we need to love and this may require an effort from us, because we may sometimes think those we need to love do not always deserve our love. None of us deserves the love of God, if God was to base His love for us on what we do. When we were yet sinners, He sent His only son to die for us. This is the expression of true love - unconditional love in the true sense. We have to extend the same kind of love to our fellow humans. You may agree that if true love were practiced as much it is sang about, this world would have been more pleasant than it is. Make the effort to love, even those who do not like you.

You Have Received The Gift of Time

This is of essence as builders of our lives and of others. This is a commodity though intangible can be measured in various forms depending on the index used, such as work and so on. We have received time as a gift from God to manage. Like various gifts we receive, it is meant to help others and ourselves in the building up of our lives. Time is defined as a non-spatial continuum in which events occur apparently in irreversible succession from the past through the present to the future[40].

We would examine a few characteristics or nature of time:

Nature One: Time is Not Static

Your life must be lived within a certain period given by God. He has given us seventy years and we may wish for more, so we can create time to carry out the things we have to accomplish. However, we can apply to our lives what we do in accounting, to give a depreciation value to our assets. This is done in order to be able to adequately plan for their replacement and to know the overall net-worth of our business. Do we do the same with our lives not that serious? Every second, minute and day of our lives leaves you with less time for existence here on this planet. The question is how well are you managing the events, situation and circumstances of your life to get a real value of the time spent? We are carrying dreams and destinies waiting to be fulfilled, when are they going to be a reality? You do not have all the time to yourself because no one can ever hog time. You dream of investing for your children, or get that degree you always yearned for, when are you going to them done? The time is now; there is no better time than you have now. Take some strides at least towards your dreams and fulfil them.

Nature Two: Time in Itself is Neutral

Your action within the space of time produces a particular result that can be measured to ascertain its value. Time in itself is neutral. Time in itself does not make anyone rich or poor, ignorant or knowledgeable. It is the activity within the space of time that defines its worth. For some, existence is just so painful, due to life's experiences whilst others see time differently. For time to be productive, some sort of value must be added to it. If you study with your time, eventually time becomes knowledge, which may get you a career in the end. Get your hands on something productive so that time can be valuable for you and others who seek it.

Nature Three: Time Is A Continuum

Time is not affected by our activities, but our activities are influenced by time. The other way to say this is that we have no influence on time either to slow it down or to stop it. To be progressive accordingly we need to keep in step with the things we are supposed to do in order to create a poise between the time we have left for ourselves and the things that needs to be done. This is not meant to make anyone rush in life but on the basis that our use of time is a crucial part of building our lives.

You Have Received The Gift Of Life

I beseech you therefore, brethren, by the mercies of God, that you present your bodies a living sacrifice, holy, acceptable to God, which is your reasonable service. (Romans 12:1-1)

Life is a gift given to humans by God with the opportunity to live in it. Life in itself is immortal because it is the part of God in us. Our body is mortal and finite. In the scripture above, the word, 'bodies' represents the totality of ones life. Your body is only the vehicle of expression that holds together your constituents. Your life consists among other things, finances, educations, relationships; sense of worth, values, ethics, marriage and beliefs. As stewards of the lives we have, we cannot therefore do anything we like with it without the approval of the one who has given it.

You cannot say 'it is my money, I choose to use it anyway I want'. You choose to use it the way God wants. Visit the money saving code, the bible to be instructed.

You cannot say 'it is my life; I choose to end it or continue with it'. The life in you that makes it possible for you to giggle, love, et cetera is not yours. If anyone chooses to end a life, even his or her own life, he or she has committed murder in the sight of God.

God Chooses Your Life to Live Through It

Your body houses the Spirit of God, so He can work through you, to accomplish His purposes here on earth. You cannot profane it. You cannot sleep with anything in skirt or trousers because you are an adult; furthermore, it is consensual and does not hurt any one. It hurts God and defiles His dwelling place. Some of us have a tradition of taking our shoes off before entering a temple, chapel or church, we even sometimes bow. These are temples made of human hands, and yet we learn to keep it respectable. We are admonished to keep our bodies clean all the time.

Aside these general gifts which we've all received according to the manifold grace of God, there are others that are specific to who we are and the assignments we need to fulfil.

These gifts are meant to serve the purposes of God by using them to bless humanity. This includes our lives as found in Romans 12:1. However, sometimes we are confronted with some issues that become the hindrances to using the grace given to us by God.

Hindrances to Using The manifold Grace of God

Hindrance One:

When You have fear of the non-existence of Heaven and Hell.

What if I do all these things and after all die only to realize that heaven and hell does not exist? You do not lose anything, in comparison to the magnitude of the pain, anguish and disappointment you will experience should they be real. It is definitive from the holy writ that these two places are real and do exist. And there are laid down criteria for those who shall go to each of these places.

Hindrance Two: The Fear of God not Stepping in on Time

Well, He does not disappoint those who put their trust in Him. There is this story about three Hebrew men who the king of Babylon sought to kill because they did not bow to worship the effigy of the king that had been made (see Daniel 3:16-18). The outcome of that story was that they did not die after being hurled into the burning furnace. The king confessed he saw another person like the son of God in the fire. A confirmation of God's Word in Isaiah 43:2, that when we go through h the fire and the water He is with us, through them all. You can rely on God. Trust in Him to be there for you. Do not entertain any fear of God forsaking you. He will stand with you to deliver you out of all your trouble.

Hindrance Three: The fear of disappointing God

We sometimes respect and love God so much that we fear to sadden him by doing the things He would not want us to do. W ask ourselves the question, 'What if I make a commitment today to submit and surrender my entire life to Him, and not able to live for Him?' He will not disappoint you. Apart from children, even adults sometimes slip and fall, but they rise up and move on. You can make it.

Watch These Things

As expressed in the first few paragraphs of this chapter, it is one thing building and another sustaining that which you build. Constructing a structure takes a definite time to build. Like most things in life, a vision, a family, moral values, career, relationships and so on, sustaining the building in the form or almost in the same shape, form, quality and quantity, takes the entire life span of the structure. Neglect of any part of this particular stage brings about decay and a total debacle or even inhabited by squatters. We would examine a story that teaches principles that would give us the knowledge and practical implementation process at the stage of our lives when we need to do a good preservation job on the things we strive to build in life.

Against Kedar and against the kingdoms of Hazor, which Nebuchadnezzar king of Babylon shall strike. Thus says the LORD: " Arise, go up to Kedar, And devastate the men of the East! Their tents and their flocks they shall take away. They shall take for themselves their curtains, all their vessels and their camels; and they shall cry out to them, 'Fear is on every side!' "Flee, get far away! Dwell in the depths, O inhabitants of Hazor!" says the LORD. "For Nebuchadnezzar king of Babylon has taken counsel against you, And has conceived a plan against you. " Arise, go up to the wealthy nation that dwells securely," says the LORD, " Which has neither gates nor bars, Dwelling alone. Their camels shall be for booty, And the multitude of their cattle for plunder. I will scatter to all winds those in the farthest corners, And I will bring their calamity from all its sides," says the LORD. "Hazor shall be a dwelling for jackals, a desolation forever; No one shall reside there, Nor son of man dwell in it." (Jeremiah 49:28-33)

God sent His prophet to prophesy against two nations; Kedar who was a desert nomadic people and Hazor, who was tax or custom and excise duties collectors. Hazor was on the trade route between Egypt and Babylon. They are described as wealthy people and people of great accomplishments. However, somewhere along the line, they could not keep up with their accomplishments. Their agency for sustaining their accomplishments developed three main flaws, and it was for this reason that they would be destroyed.

- **They dwell securely (at ease, without care) – Complacency**

- **They have neither gates nor bars – Security**

- **They dwell alone – Isolation**

The flaws revealed in the scripture are complacency, security and isolation. Let us probe these flaws as to how they subverted the accomplishments of Kedar and Hazor.

Flaw One: Complacency

Life is not a dress rehearsal, everyday is your day of performance therefore there is no room for complacency. You will need to put in many efforts for whatever your hand finds to do at anytime. Each day has a link with your future. There is no other day the same as the other. There were 53 Mondays in 2007, but they are all different. With the passing of each day, the chronometer of your life is ticking and there is never going to be a recurrence of wasted time. Arise and accomplish great things with your life, but more so sustain what you build in life. Let us read David's prayer:

"O God, You have taught me from my youth; and to this day I declare Your wondrous works. 18 Now also when I am old and grayheaded, O God, do not forsake me, Until I declare Your strength to this generation, Your power to everyone who is to come." (Psalm 71:17)

This prayer is from a heart that is leaning on leaving a legacy for the generation after him. He was a content man but not a complacent man. A content person acknowledges what God has done and introspectively considers where he had come from and what is left to be achieved. A complacent person says 'I'm alright. I need no more'. David says my experience has been good in the past and there is evidence to show, but I need more for prospective generations.

Complacency is self-satisfaction, particularly

when accompanied by unawareness of actual dangers or deficiencies. Complacency made Kedar loose sight of the most important issues of security and isolation. It is interesting to note that not only was complacency the problem of Old Testament times, New Testament but also a contemporary problem.

We sometimes get too complacent too soon with a little achievement. It looks as if success itself is an enemy of success for many people. You get a spouse, a nice car, a beautiful family, a beautiful family home, and soon we lose any stimulus to accomplish anything more or sustain, that which has been achieved over time.

Look Beyond Yourself

Do not let your motivation, enthusiasm and drive to accomplish more be influenced by your experiences. Norman Cousins (an accomplished author and editor) says 'death is not the greatest loss of life. The greatest loss is what dies inside us while we live'. Until your achievement, affect the life of others beyond yourself and immediate family. Therefore, arise and carry on achieving.

Sources of Complacency and Their Remedy

Source One:

When There Are Too Many Perceived Resources

We tend to be complacent when there are too many perceived resources. Anytime people have too many choices they tend not to strive for more. You may know it is difficult to choose a dress for a charity ball or any other highly valued occasion when there are about a hundred or more outfits. Some affluent people even employ others to handle their wardrobe.

Beware that you do not forget the LORD your God by not keeping His commandments, His judgments, and His statutes which I command you today, lest— when you have eaten and are full, and have built beautiful houses and dwell in them; and when your herds and your flocks multiply, and your silver and your gold are multiplied, and all that you have is multiplied; when your heart is lifted up, and you forget the LORD your God who brought you out of the land of Egypt, from the house of bondage; (Deuteronomy 8:11-14)

God commands the people should be circumspect not to deny His existence when all their needs are met. It is easy to be self-satisfied when there are no external needs. You tend not to strive for any further.

David perceived this danger, and so He prayed to God not to give him too many resources, to make him complacent in his service to God or even deny the existence of God. In the western world or rich countries of the world young people of school going age are practically motivated to go to school, which is free, yet some of these young people still ignore these leading. There are others in the developing world where there are no schools, and those who intend to go to school would have to travel across five to ten miles to get to the nearest school. In some of these countries, education is purely a privilege. There is nothing wrong with having too many visible resources but when they become the reason, you no longer strive further to accomplish anything or to sustain that which has already been built, this can be extremely dangerous.

Source Two: When There Are No Major Visible Crisis

It is interesting that even in the house of God, there are people who do not come to church when all is well with them. You only see them when an unfortunate situation has befallen them. Either a relative of theirs is dead, or they are in church for the funeral service or have personally been struck by some vicissitude. It was partly the reason God decided to leave pockets of tribes of Israel enemy states in the promise land. Therefore, they would remain alert. The rationale was to prevent them, being out-numbered by the animals in the areas where they had settled.

You Develop Creativity in Crisis

But the LORD your God will deliver them over to you, and will inflict defeat upon them until they are destroyed. (Deuteronomy 7:23)

Crisis sometimes keeps people thinking, planning and moving forward, generally in life. Susan Taylor once said that 'Seeds of faith are always within us; sometimes it takes a crisis to nourish and encourage their growth'. This is about the positive thing about crisis, it is said that necessity is the mother of invention. Most innovation has come about as a solution to an existing problem. Countries that have been through times of depression have come out much stronger and prosperous than they were before. The human nature is such that it does not want to be suppressed; we all tend to want to bounce back during crises. It is an unfortunate assertion to make about human nature that the absence of a major and visible crisis tends to make us complacent. We however do not have to wait to be struck with a crisis before you arise to accomplish something in life or sustain what you have achieved in the past.

Source Three: When There Is No Sufficient Performance Feedback From External Sources

An Akan (Ghanaian Language) that says, 'he who cuts the path forward without looking back sometimes wouldn't know the path is getting crooked behind him'. That is to say that you need people's appraisal to ascertain you are still on course. There are times however that everyone is wrong, and you are right. The majority is not always right. The person who first postulated the earth was not flat but in the shape, we all now know it to be was placed under house arrest[41], because he could not show evidence to back up his claims. In spite of the fact that, the majority's voice is not always the voice of God, there are times people see things that is impossible to see yourself. People are inclined to be self-conceited and loose the edge for further achievements and sustaining their achievements.

Take Criticisms In Good Faith

Sometimes we fear people criticising our work, activities or actions and as a result are very uncomfortable to seek other's opinion of what we do. There are times we do this because it makes us feel little in the eyes of those who see the faults or areas that need amelioration. It is either pride or a low self-esteem in us being displayed. The best situation would be to get a matured, trustworthy individual who can be objective, yet put across his or her views in a way that encourages you and not demoralise you. Whatever you build in life, as revealed earlier that is not solely for us but for others, so that in many situations, others apart from us can have an opinion of our work based on how it affects them. For instance, a person trains to be a teacher, not to teach himself or herself but others. It is those he or she teaches who determines whether he or she is a good teacher.

How To Remedy Complacency

Remedy One:

Develop Internal Measurements Systems That Focus on Right Performance Indexes

In most work places, certain performance indexes are put in place to guide the individual to be in line with the goals of the firm for which they work. For instance, a person who may be working for a service company's complaints department may be given a task to convince about 70 out of 100 people who are unhappy with the company's services to stay on. Therefore, if these targets are met, these indexes have been observed, because they become the reference point of the success or failure of the individual on the job. This is however an external measurement system with a clear performance index.

Unfortunately, some of the things we have internalised and view as our performance index are wrong. How would you measure success, for instance is it in the number of houses a person has or how many lives you have touched by an act of kindness? Whenever our performance index is wrong, our accomplishments in themselves will be in jeopardy, because they may be worthless. This becomes a great source of complacency, which must be examined and corrected. You cannot be successful or accomplish mush when there is too much self-satisfaction but unaware of the potential dangers that can stall the building process.

Remedy Two: The Things You Consider important Must Be important To God

To correct this, we need to be able to define the things that God considers important and accordingly bring into congruence to what is important to us.

"Do not lay up for yourselves treasures on earth, where moth and rust destroy and where thieves break in and steal; However, lay up for yourselves treasures in heaven, where neither moth nor rust destroys and where thieves do not break in and steal. For where your treasure is, there your heart will be also. (Matthew 6:19-21)

Here Jesus was teaching about value systems, the fact that we need to align our value systems to that of the Kingdom of God. We can measure real success by the principles set out in God's Word. Any work or activity that does not translate into eternal rewards in heaven falls short of this standard. Aligning with God's Word guarantees eternal rewards for us. You have become complacent if the things you have and are accomplishing are not focusing on the right performance index, which is an alignment with the things God considers important in His Kingdom, those things that can translate into eternal rewards. Everything we have can actually be made to provide us with an eternal reward as they fall in line with God's approved performance index. With this in mind never again would we be complacent, because a demand for performance and true accomplishment is very high.

Remedy Three: Focus On Broader Functional Goals

Complacency sets in when the things we want to attain are narrow and not dynamic in nature to encompass areas related to our targets. A goal is no goal if it can be easily attained; it must stretch your resources, capabilities and competencies. There have been times when you realised you have not achieved anything at all after having a first hand experience of what others have done. There is no suggestion here that we can all do that another is doing, because the graces, faith and strength are not on the same levels. The challenge for a greater accomplishment by another brings it to the point of stretching yourself out to maximise your capabilities.

It is better to set functional progressive goals where you can keep pushing forward as a boost to stretch yourself, in order to reach them. We can import this idea about the way we organize our physical exercise everyday. We will agree that the number of miles we cover is not what we started with; we keep pushing it forward to creating room to develop greater endurance. Do not settle or stand still, because standing still is falling behind. Keep moving forward. Someone once said that 'life is like a bicycle, the only way you can keep it moving forward is when it is standing. You might have attained and accomplished some things in life, but there is more you can do and become.

For the reason of complacency, enemies destroyed Kedar and Hazor, although they were very wealthy and influential in their time. There is every reason why you should continue to strive forward to accomplishing more.

Flaw Two: Being Isolated

The word alone is defined as:

- to set apart from others

- to select from among others.

Isolation can be imposed such as incarceration and segregation as it was the case in apartheid South Africa. Isolation can also be voluntary. It appears from the scripture that the kind of isolation that Hazor and Kedar were caught up in were voluntary in nature. In all probability, their lifestyles were the bane of their own development. The people of Kedar were a desert nomadic people who moved from one place to the other and did not stay at one place for a time to maintain any serious social ties with surrounding cities and people. They dwelt in places where they could find pasture for their flock and for them this was their priority. They never considered the fact that we all need each other, and that they needed allies who would be a support in a case, there was an attack on them from foreign raiders, as this was common in those days.

The kind of isolation that Hazor might have been caught up in was imposed. Even in the New Testament, tax collectors were shunned and despised, to the extent that people did not want to have any association with them. It was for this reason that Jesus Christ was accused of eating with tax collectors.

You Can't Do It All By Yourself

Clearly isolation, whether voluntary or imposed has fatal consequences. God created us, so we can become interdependent on each other In other words, to accomplish your purposes in life or accomplish anything it is typically done within a context where others play one role or other to make it happen. Everybody needs somebody, and do not forget that there is nothing like 'I'm a self-made man or woman', whether in a ministry, business, family etc. The only reason you felt this way is that you have not acknowledged the people who have played diverse roles in your life. You would not be reading this book if sometime past whilst sick in bed you did not have medicine produced by the employees of a pharmaceutical company on its factory floors. Furthermore, by the shareholders who own the company and even the doctor who prescribed the medication. This may not be an adequate snapshot of the support and help we obtain from each other. I may have my name as the author of this book you are reading however there are many stories I have heard, experiences with people, interactions with people of diverse backgrounds, the influence of my mentor, biographic studies et cetera that inform and strengthen my convictions.

Allow Others to Contribute Into Your Life

They have all played a role in my life. No one would build a solid life successfully if we live in isolation of each other. One thing that we need to take in is that, we are all here on earth for a different purpose and not in competition. Life is a race where every individual has his or her own finishing line. For some, the distance to be covered is short; for others it is long, and therefore it cannot be a competition. It was a human idea to create classes among people so that others who put themselves in the higher classes can suppress those who are in the lower classes or accept their placements. It is an understatement to say that the consequences of that handiwork of man have proven to be fatal. Talk about the Rwanda genocide where Hutus the majority tribe slaughter the minority Tutsis who were considered the elites of the country, a class system created by former colonial masters. In a space of about six weeks, about 800,000 people representing a tenth of the population had been killed with machetes and clubs[42].

We Win Together, When We Run Together

You can doubtlessly guarantee there would be peace and order in our world, workplace, home if we know that we are meant to depend on each other accomplish great things in our lives. Envy, jealousy and schisms should be old-fashioned. Unhealthy competition concocts isolation; we can all accomplish great things supporting one another. It seems to me that this is the down side of the extreme application of capitalism. Nevertheless, it has indeed many positives that include entrepreneurship and rewards hardworking individuals. This has permeated almost every area of human life, even the church.

However, before then, there is this moving commercial on a news channel in the U.K. that tells a story. There were these youngsters, in a race with their parents cheering on. One of the youngsters in no time surged ahead of their colleagues by a considerable distance towards the finishing line, and then this boy tripped over and fell. He laid there sobbing while all the contestants passed him by. Unexpectedly, they all stopped, came back and held their colleague up from the ground, held hands together and crossed the line together. We are here on this planet to help each other to fulfil our purposes. Next time you have to help someone, even if it is a service for money, do it with a different attitude. Take a step now with this insight and see how you can change our world. We would look at isolation from two main perspectives; the church and society.

Do Not Isolate Yourself From Your Church

And let us consider one another in order to stir up love and good works, not forsaking the assembling of ourselves together, as is the manner of some, but exhorting one another, and so much the more as you see the Day approaching. (Hebrews 10:24-25)

You come across persons who have stopped going to church due to one situation or the other, and claim that they are serving God in their hearts. As much as the condition of the heart is important in our worship to God, it is equally significant to belong to an assembly of believers. You may know that some professions have societies, which every individual in that profession must belong. They govern the activities of these professionals, to provide support and seek ways to develop further the profession to meet human requirements and industry standards by keeping them apposite to the times.

Similarly, believers are not to forsake the assembly of themselves together. As you go to church, you are edified, encouraged and strengthened (see Proverbs 27:17). Offence is inevitable where there are other human beings. Forgiveness would heal all offences, if we allow forgiveness space in our lives. What we need to understand is that no human institution with all its efficiencies is perfect.

Reach Out! Someone Needs You

In relation to attending church as admonished by the writer of Hebrews, our commitment to the responsibilities within our churches is worthy of note. It is a shame that there are people who may belong to your church and yet cannot find someone to speak to, apart from the Pastor or ministry leader. Some of us have built walls around us by walking, talking, dressing and acting in a particular way to make it impossible for others to break into us. Unfortunately, that makes it even impossible for God to break into us. You want to reach out to someone. Do not look any further. The person who may be sitting in the next pew may be in need. Reach out to someone today, this week, and this month. How else can you say, you love God and yet do not love your fellow humans. For anyone who is genuinely close to God is so close to people, in other words cares about people.

John the Baptist was one such person who seemed to have separated himself from people, spent time in isolation in the desert waiting upon God, and yet it is from the wilderness that he preached his message of repentance and the Kingdom of God. He cared about people, although he seemed to have been isolated from people to spend time with God in the wilderness. The early church grew because they were together and more so cared for each other (see Acts 2:46-47).

Don't Stay Marginalised In Society

There are many factors that contribute to isolation as far as social development is concerned, this includes disability (as in many developing countries) racial discrimination among others. The scripture below provides us with a classic example;

But Solomon took thirteen years to build his own house; so he finished all his house. He also built the House of the Forest of Lebanon; its length was one hundred cubits, its width fifty cubits, and its height thirty cubits, with four rows of cedar pillars, and cedar beams on the pillars. And it was paneled with cedar above the beams that were on forty-five pillars, fifteen to a row. There were windows with beveled frames in three rows, and window was opposite window in three tiers. And all the doorways and doorposts had rectangular frames; and window was opposite window in three tiers. He also made the Hall of Pillars: its length was fifty cubits, and its width thirty cubits; and in front of them was a portico with pillars, and a canopy was in front of them. Then he made a hall for the throne, the Hall of Judgment, where he might judge; and it was paneled with cedar from floor to ceiling. And the house where he dwelt had another court inside the hall, of like workmanship. Solomon also made a house like this hall for Pharaoh's daughter, whom he had taken as a wife. All these were of costly stones cut to size, trimmed with saws, inside and out, from the foundation to the eaves, and also on the outside to the great court. The foundation was of costly stones, large stones, some ten cubits and some eight cubits. And above were costly stones, hewn to size, and cedar wood.(1 Kings 7:1-11)

The above scripture gives reasons why these lepers were relegated to the fringes of life. You can imagine the enormity of their plight even those in the town centre where the food distribution chain begins were hungry. They would have been indeed in great distress not only from the hunger but from the fact that they could not freely go into the town centre to get the portion they so desire for themselves. This was so because they had leprosy and according to their local laws, those with this disease face social exclusion. As mentioned there are many people in very prosperous countries and communities who are excluded from partaking of the available resources meant for the entire populace.

Your Efforts Would Be Magnified

What is absorbing in this story is the act of God's divine grace of choosing these lepers to be the ones through whom the abundance of food predicted by Elisha in the previous chapter materialises? God indeed chooses the foolish things of the world to confound the wise. At that moment when they had gone to the town centre to announce how God had confused the enemy by amplifying the sound of their footsteps to make the enemy flee; thinking it was a mighty army, their leprosy did not matter anymore. It seems to me that social solitariness occurs to an individual or people whom others cannot consider to be deserving of the same privileges and rights they enjoy.

Flaw Three: Security

It is amazing how these successful wealthy people did not build any form of security to predispose them to enemy invasions. Many nations spend a great deal of money on providing safety to their people. In the war against terror with the aim of making the United States of America safe, many billions are spent each year to keep this operation going. In fact, security is a human need and without it, few things can be accomplished in life.

Protect What You Build

In the theory of motivation developed by Abraham Maslow, in his Hierarchy of Needs illustration, in matter of succession, he has physiological needs at the bottom of the ladder, followed by safety needs, belonging and love needs, esteem needs and then self-actualization needs[43] in that order. The summary of this theory is that in the order of importance, people would only seek things bottom-up. That is to say that, the issue of security for instance is so important that people do not look for self-actualisation or avenues to be useful to society until their security needs have been met. Jesus stressed the need for security in the scripture.

And Jesus said to him, "Foxes have holes and birds of the air have nests, but the Son of Man has nowhere to lay His head." (Mathew 8: 20)

In other words, would you deprive yourself of a basic need of humanity to follow me? For this statement, some people stopped following him. It is true to say that when you take some of the poor countries of the world you will realise that they are not even thinking about going to the moon when they have problems with food security. There's not a single year where there are no food shortfalls and hikes in food prices due to lack of proper storage, transportation and efficient regulatory bodies to regulate food prices among others. At this point, of development going to the moon is not a priority.

Be Spiritually Secured

If anyone is in Christ, he or she is into a covenant with God through Christ. This is because Christ had come to die and sacrifice himself for us;

His blood is what has paid the price for the cost of our deliverance from Satan's authority and restoring us into our bona fide place in the creation of God. The scriptures say without the shedding of blood, there is no forgiveness of sin (see Hebrews 9:22). The blood of Jesus forms the basis of our covenant with God. It is for this reason that He says;

There is therefore now no condemnation to those who are in Christ Jesus, who do not walk according to the flesh, but according to the Spirit. For the law of the Spirit of life in Christ Jesus has made me free from the law of sin and death. For what the law could not do in that it was weak through the flesh, God did by sending His own Son in the likeness of sinful flesh, on account of sin: He condemned sin in the flesh, that the righteous requirement of the law might be fulfilled in us who do not walk according to the flesh but according to the Spirit (Romans 8:1-4)

We have been preferred over others; we enjoy security that protects us from Satan's devices against us, we are the focus of attention above everything else. Therefore, if you are in Christ, you enjoy supernatural protection of God from any form of encroachment meant to destroy your life or cut short your life's dreams and purposes is dealt with. We have a responsibility to keep ourselves within the boundaries of God's love by walking in obedience to His will. Always remember this verse from Ecclesiastes 10:8b. "And whoever breaks through a wall will be bitten by a serpent"

Get Financial Security

We work laboriously and have been doing so, for the past few years, and yet have nothing to show for it. You want to understand why your finances are in a mess. Apart from pecuniary mismanagement, the neglect of God's principle of tithing and neglect of the needs of the house of God is also a cause of the fiscal mess. Many of us buy things we do not need. I once chanced upon a program on a station on the Sky Broadcasting Networking while channel surfing, where people are encouraged to sell things they've bought and have slightly used or not used at all. Easy access to cash on plastics has made it easy to buy things either on the street or at home and literally anywhere. This has made it easy for those who want every new model of electronic gadgets launched although they may have the previous model.

'Things' Cannot Boost Your Sense Of Worth

You need to grasp that one of the indicators of low self-esteem is when you depend on anything outside yourself to derive a sense of worth. This condition is what makes people break their bank accounts and misuse their credit card funds to buy designer products their earnings cannot sustain. We need to bear in mind that wearing a particular designer outfit does not make you the designer himself or herself. You also do not get equal in bank balance with rich celebrity whom you are emulating. Preferably of undertake some investments in order to lock up the value of your money and even multiply it. Cut down on your spending, as expressed earlier, you are not in competition with anyone. Be yourself, live according to the available resources to you.

Give To Your Local Assembly of Believers

It is interesting to discover that not all issues of financial lack are caused by mismanagement but our dereliction of duty to God's house can create situation through which we lose funds. Maintaining a place where many come to seek the face of Jehovah is His delight. We cannot ourselves be living comfortably when a designated place as the house of God lies ignored. Consider your ways and do that which is right in the sight of God. When it comes to giving to the house of God, the principal thing believers of both the Old and New Testament was instructed to do, was to give to the work of the Gospel that proceeded from the pastoral office. The Old Testament believers were commanded to tithe and this was used to support the Levites and priests in their work of service before God (see Numbers 18:20-24; Deuteronomy 14:22; 26:12; 2 Chronicle 31:1-20; Hebrews 7:5).

In the New Testament, various scriptures admonish us to support the appointed Minister and the ministry. 'Let him who is taught the word share in all good things with him who teaches' (Galatians 6:6); Furthermore, 'do you not know that those who minister the holy things eat of the things of the temple, and those who serve at the altar partake of the offering of the altar? Even so the Lord has commanded that those who preach the gospel should live from the gospel' (see 1 Corinthians 9:13-14). Let the elders who rule well be counted worthy of double honour, especially those who labour in the word and doctrine. For the scripture says, 'you shall not muzzle an ox while it treads out the grain' and, and 'the labourer is worthy of his wages' (1 Timothy 5:17-18).

Your Giving Pushes The Gospel Where You Cannot Reach Physically

From the above scriptures Christians must give so that Christian pastors, missionaries and congregation have what they need to preach the gospel. What we need to understand is that ministry work as the Lord Jesus committed to us, has become more intricate just as the structure of society has become and is becoming more complex by the day. TV programs are aired to homes across the world where you would other wise not reach in person. Programs are initiated for clothing those in need of clothing, feeding the peckish caring for those in jail, getting the youth out of the streets from gun crime, drug-dealing prostitution among others. No doubt it takes money to do ministry work and ministry is about reaching out with the love of God in Christ giving himself up to die in our place, that through him, we may have eternal life.

Keep Yours But Give To God What Is His First

In the Old Testament, God's people gave God a tenth of their increase, known as the tithe. Abraham gave to Melchizedek, priest of the Most High God (whom the Book of Hebrews refers to as God himself) a tenth of the spoils from his victory over the kings from Mesopotamia region (Genesis 14:20). Jacob promised God a tithe of his wealth if He would protect and bless him (Genesis28:22). The Law of Moses made tithing a compulsory element in the worship of God for the people of Israel (Leviticus 27:30-32; Deuteronomy 14:22-23). Malachi also rebuked the population for not walking in obedience of God's command of tithing and described the acts of neglect as robbery.

The New Testament however does not have any commandment to tithe. The reason is that, the law of tithing is one of Old Testament laws that the church retained in principle, just like the observance of the Sabbath. Jesus mentions tithe in the gospels (see Matthew 23:23), in His warning to the religious leaders at the time, reinforcing the fact that it was an accepted law practiced by the church. In the scripture Jesus did not condemn tithing but rather the fact that all the things God commands are to be kept and practiced, and none should be raised above the other while others are neglected.

Many believers have their liquidity in disarray also because they have neglected the needs of the house of God from where the gospel is prepared.

Thus speaks the LORD of hosts, saying: 'This people says, "The time has not come, the time that the LORD's house should be built."'" Then the word of the LORD came by Haggai the prophet, saying, "Is it time for you yourselves to dwell in your paneled houses, and this temple to lie in ruins?" Now therefore, thus says the LORD of hosts: "Consider your ways!(Haggai 1:2-5)

Connect Yourself To Endless Divine Supplies

Tithing makes a divine connection with the sources of all wealth. The tithe becomes the conduit through which His provisions would flow into your life. One of the things tithing does is to assist you to open up your mind to life changing ideas. Many exceptionally wealthy people attribute their financial success to among other things tithing. Many people have realized that through tithing, they live more abundantly and all their needs are met more easily. With plenty left over. I have read many books on success and personal development and what surprises me is that I do not know much about the spiritual background of these writers until I come across a paragraph or section that talks about giving and paying of tithe. These men and women are successful; people and apart from being a person who tithe it reinforces my conviction that if these people are successful then it is worth holding on to these truths. All these are for the contemporary times such as it was done in the Old Testament. Let us look at a practical guideline on tithing;

Practice One: Start paying your tithe immediately

If only you earn an income, you have to start paying immediately. Do not allow your tithe to accumulate over a period. To help you be faithful, pay on the next Sunday you receive your income as delay may entice you to expend it.

Practice Two: Your Tithe Must Be Real Tithe

Tithe should be on your gross income. Every deduction from your income is no less yours because you never see it. Monies deducted are payments for benefits you receive in return. Benefits that include retirement income, medical care and other governmental services supported are by taxes. In some cases, student loans are also taken out of income before you are actually paid. Therefore, paying your tithe on your net pay is not accurate since that does not represent your actual income.

Practice Three: Consider Paying Your Tithe First

Consider paying your tithe before handling your bills to avoid your bills taking all the money, with nothing left for tithe.

God promises material blessing among other things for His people. However, our desire should not be for the selfish benefits because this is wrong in the sight of God.

The reason why you would give your tithe is that you love God. As you give to Him, you show that you appreciate what He has done for you.

Develop A New Lifestyle For Every New Challenge

Then the disciples of John came to Him, saying, "Why do we and the Pharisees fast often, but Your disciples do not fast?"
And Jesus said to them, "Can the friends of the bridegroom mourn as long as the bridegroom is with them? But the days will come when the bridegroom will be taken away

from them, and then they will fast. No one puts a piece of unshrunk cloth on an old garment; for the patch pulls away from the garment, and the tear is made worse. Nor do they put new wine into old wineskins, or else the wineskins break, the wine is spilled, and the wineskins are ruined. But they put new wine into new wineskins, and both are preserved."(Matthew 9:14-17)

The above scripture accentuates the thought expressed in the entire section. Jesus in the context of these verses was teaching about His presence in the world, that He had not come to patch up an old system, like sewing a new unshrunk cloth to an old garment, which would tear. Furthermore, like pouring new wine into an old wine skin, this would burst. He had come to lead people who believe in Him into a kingdom based on Him and His righteousness. In this analogy of the wine skins, you have to comprehend that, in the Bible eras wine was not kept in glass bottles but in goatskins sewn around the edges to form watertight bags. The new wine expanded as it ferments, stretching its wine skin, so that if new wine is poured into old wine skin, it would burst with the procedure because it would have reached its elastic limits. It simply cannot handle the process of fermentation where gases are released to produce pressure in the wine skin.

Develop The Mind Set Of Maintenance

By application, the new wine is our achievements; the things we produce with our lives. The wine skins are containers – lifestyles with which we hold the things we produce with our lives. Therefore, the new wine skins are an adaptable lifestyle, which is a way of life that reflects the aggregate of the lessons you have learnt from your experiences, internalised information, beliefs and value systems that informs your actions.

Anyone seeking to sustain his or her accomplishments would need a lifestyle alteration. It is obvious that some things are difficult to change than others but if what we have accomplished is important to us then we need to pay the price to sustain it. The truth is that, the lifestyle disposition you need whilst building is different as what we needed in the maintenance. You need a new set of information, mindset, attitude and behavioural pattern at this particular stage.

It is now evident that what caused the anger of God for an imminent demise of two great cities; Hazor and Kedar are of contemporary application because we have developed the same faults within our mechanisms for accomplishments. As we change our ways through soul-searching and thorough evaluation of our lifestyles we would be able to sustain any accomplishments we have made by the grace of

God.

A man builds a fine house; and now he has a master, and a task for life; he is to furnish, watch, show it, and keep it in repair, the rest of his days.
-Ralph Waldo Emerson

7

OBSERVING THE FULL SABBATH: RESTING FROM ALL YOUR WORKS

Laziness is nothing more than the habit of resting before you get tired. **-Jules Renard**

If you have ever been to a construction site, you will find that the builders take rest. There is not a condition where they build deprived of taking some time off to rest. The rest provides them with the opportunity to regain their strength and return to work. This is to avert burn out and to enable the builder manage the stress of the building process. This is not different from life building.

The word Sabbath in the Hebrew means to cease or

to stop. The Sabbath begins from the night of Friday through the Saturday. The Sabbath is the reminder of two great truths: Creation and Redemption. Of creation, the Sabbath commemorates God's creation rest on the seventh day. It marks a finished creation.

Of redemption, when God brought Israel out of Egypt after Sinai, He gave them the law to keep as a matter of obligation.

"The Sabbath is mentioned often in the book of Acts about the Jews. In the rest of the New Testament, it occurs twice;

So let no one judge you in food or in drink, or regarding a festival or a new moon or sabbaths, (Colossians 2:16)

For He has spoken in a certain place of the seventh day in this way: "And God rested on the seventh day from all His works" (Hebrews 4:4)

You Rest From Your Works When You Believe In The Lord

In these passages, the Sabbath is set forth not as a day to be observed but as typical of the contemporary rest into which the believer enters when he rests from his works and trusts in Christ. That is to say, that when a person believes in Christ, they have fulfilled the law of obligatory rest, since he has taken over the effort to please God by dying to save us. There are three main expanses for works: rest from our works- sin, rest from works- salvation and rest from works- needs.

In a summary, because we believe in Jesus, he has given us rest from carrying our sins, the burden to please God by our works, and has taken over the responsibility of providing our needs. These were all personified in the promulgation made whilst on the cross at Calvary;

So when Jesus had received the sour wine, He said, "It is finished!" And bowing His head, He gave up His spirit. (John 19:30)

Life building can from time to time be murky due to its very complex nature. However, resting mean God taking over and carrying our burdens in the process. In the scripture quoted above, Jesus meant your court case, is finished, your failure is finished, your aliment, your debt, divorce, poverty, suborn child, in that every unfavourable and injurious situation you should be worried about has been taken care of. For us believers, this is the real quintessence of being in Christ. It is no longer just the physical observation of rest but of spiritual significance as well.

Learn to Turn Over Your Burdens To Him

When we cede to build up our lives in God, through Christ, He takes over and gives us rest. Observing the Sabbath in the New Testament era is totally yielding our lives and the building process to Christ allowing Him to take charge of all the trials, difficulties and apprehensions. There is no need to continue to carry this process by your strength if there is help on hand in Christ. It is very important to acknowledge that the supreme architect – God, has provided the design we are building for us therefore in any corporeal construction of a building, the architect is involved from beginning to the end to make sure that the outcome is a refection of the design. We cannot all do it by our strength and our might, but by the spirit of God.

You Cannot Do It All By Your Strength

The Holy Spirit enables us to accomplish what we are unable to do with our own resolve. Inasmuch as he gives the assignment, He does not leave us alone but gives us his Spirit to provide us with the enablement to do so. We will look at stories from the Old Testament and the New Testament to explain this point.

So he answered and said to me:
"This is the word of the LORD to Zerubbabel:
'Not by might nor by power, but by My Spirit,'
Says the LORD of hosts.
' Who are you, O great mountain?
Before Zerubbabel you shall become a plain!
And he shall bring forth the capstone
With shouts of "Grace, grace to it!"'"(Zechariah 4:6-7)

God had given an assignment to Zerrubabel who at the time was a governor of Jerusalem. Zerubbabel had led the first colony of captives to Jerusalem accompanied by Joshua the high priest, Levites, and heads of houses of Judah and Benjamin. Arriving at Jerusalem, their first task was to build the altar on its old site and to restore the daily sacrifice.

However, the task had not advanced when the mixed settlers in Samaria put in a claim to take part of it. Zerrubbabel and his associates declined the offer, they – mixed settlers in Samaria endeavoured to encumber the completion of the Temple. As a result, the work was suspended, although the hardships in the way of the Temple did not require a cessation of work. It was at this moment that God spoke to Zerrubbabel telling him, 'it's not by might nor by power but by the spirit'.

In other words, until He enables Zerrubbabel with His Spirit's power upon him, the project was bound to fail. As we saw in the scripture, the work came to a stand still due to the confrontation from the mixed settlers in Samaria. We can with the Holy Spirit reach higher heights, build our lives with joy, and thrill to God's approval.

You Will Become Another Person

We have been talking about how we could build our lives successfully. The essence of this is to become what God has empowered us to be. We have seen that when the spirit of God comes upon us, we can accomplish any tasks He gives us. God's ultimate plan for giving such a message to Zerrubabel was to bring about a change in His thinking and attitude that would in turn affect the building. Since we are the builders and the building ourselves, experiencing any form of transformation is to both the building and the builder.

We can learn from the story of Samuels anointing of Saul as King of Israel below;

After that you shall come to the hill of God where the Philistine garrison is. And it will happen, when you have come there to the city, that you will meet a group of prophets coming down from the high place with a stringed instrument, a tambourine, a flute, and a harp before them; and they will be prophesying. Then the Spirit of the LORD will come upon you, and you will prophesy with them and be turned into another man. (1 Samuel 10:5-6)

When they came there to the hill, there was a group of prophets to meet him; then the Spirit of God came upon him, and he prophesied among them. And it happened, when all who knew him formerly saw that he indeed prophesied among the prophets, that the people said to one another, "What is this that has come upon the son of Kish? Is Saul also among the prophets?" Then a man from there answered and said, "But who is their father?" Therefore it became a proverb: "Is Saul also among the prophets?" And when he had finished prophesying, he went to the high place.(1 Samuel 10:10-13)

The awe-inspiring thing is that, the prophecy of Samuel shortly came about after the anointing, and when Saul began prophesying with the group of prophets, persons who saw him, asked whether he was also among the prophets. The reason for that query was that they knew Saul quite well and probably as a matter of course there was no way he could prophesy and here was Saul prophesying. Undoubtedly, Saul had become another person because the spirit of God had come upon him. In other words, the Spirit of God became the differentiation between Saul's previous abilities and life as a whole and the current one.

Display Your Transformation

The finished work of a building cannot be hidden; all its pomp, grandeur and imperfection are in the open for people to judge.

At the arrest, trial and crucifixion of Jesus some of His disciples were traumatized and others openly denied Him. In spite of this, Jesus encouraged them to gather in one place until they received the Holy Spirit with power because they could not carry out their ministry without the Holy Spirit. This is what happened;

So they were all amazed and perplexed, saying to one another, "Whatever could this mean?" Others mocking said, "They are full of new wine. But Peter, standing up with the eleven, raised his voice and said to them, "Men of Judea and all who dwell in Jerusalem, let this be known to you, and heed my words. For these are not drunk, as you suppose, since it is only the third hour of the day. (Acts 2:12-15)

Some of the adherents and apostles were the same fearful, timid people known by everyone until the Holy Spirit was poured upon their lives. They at this moment in time have the temerity to proclaim Jesus as Lord.

This was a great display of transformation within a short space of time.

Your Transformation Would Always Astound People

The staggering thing is that whilst this was happening, the audience thought they were intoxicated, they could hear them in their own languages. That was the only way they could explain what they were seeing. In fact, they are not to be upbraided, because someone had to find a way to explain what looked like an abnormality. They were certainly under some kind on influence to be able to do that. Furthermore, this they thought was alcohol, but it was the influence of the Holy Spirit. Any real achievement we can ever experience is a transformation of our lives. A change that others can recognize originates from God. We can make significant strides towards becoming what we are all meant to be by inviting the Holy Spirit into our lives. The Holy Spirit will not only come to heal you, speak in tongues or display the gifts of the spirit but also help you in your day-to-day building up of your life. Maybe you are saying I am too old to implement and apply the principles you have read, that may be wrong because this is just about the right time to start applying these principles. You may have tried many other things that have not worked.

This Stuff Works

This is an invitation to arise, embrace the supreme architect into your life, and give Him the opportunity to transform you as He has done in millions of lives around the world. It is only at this point that life would take on a dramatic turn and meaning.

The reason people could accomplish great things in life, and are still not fulfilled is mainly that we tend to think things could seal the void we have in our lives, which only God in Christ can fill.

We face challenges, as we build our lives, but we can overcome following the principles God has explicitly made clear in His Word. We would not only overcome our difficulties and hindrances but also be able to sustain and provide maintenance for the life we build. Let us build and wait for our commendation from our architect.

EPILOGUE

We sometimes give up in trying again due to the difficulties and snags we face in the process of building our lives. It does not matter if you gave up on your life some years, months, weeks or days ago, you can start all over again. Like the story we read from Mark 5:21- 43 about the ruler of the synagogue, whilst he was on his way, home with Jesus Christ to heal his daughter, there were interferences that caused a delay. A certain woman touched Jesus and Jesus stopped to have a discourse with those around Him, in the end, a report came from the ruler's house that his daughter was dead. Maybe you had a similar experience where everything was functioning properly well until something suddenly took place and crushed your dreams or even diminished your energy to keep building your life.

You Can Start All Over Again.

The word which came to Jeremiah from the LORD, saying: "Arise and go down to the potter's house, and there I will cause you to hear My words." Then I went down to the potter's house, and there he was, making something at the wheel. And the vessel that he made of clay was marred in the hand of the potter; so he made it again into another vessel, as it seemed good to the potter to make.
  Then the word of the LORD came to me, saying: "O house of Israel, can I not do with you as this potter?" says the LORD. "Look, as the clay is in the potter's hand, so are you in My hand, O house of Israel! The instant I speak concerning a nation and concerning a kingdom, to pluck up, to pull down, and to destroy it, if that nation against whom I have spoken turns from its evil, I will relent of the disaster that I thought to bring upon it. And the instant I speak concerning a nation and concerning a kingdom, to build and to plant it, if it does evil in My sight so that it does not obey My voice, then I will relent concerning the good with which I said I would benefit it. (Jeremiah 18:1-10)

God wanted to speak to his people through the Prophet Jeremiah but to make an impression upon him for a better understanding, He asked him to go to the potter's house. In The Potter's house according to Jeremiah, the clay, the potter was moulding got marred in his hands, but he made it again into another vessel. Consequently, the Word of the Lord was, 'cannot I do the same with you?' The simple lesson here is this, we are the clay in the hands of the potter, God, and when by some means or unfortunate situation, we are marred in His hands; He can make us into another vessel.

Sometimes we give up on our lives when God is getting ready to bless us. The fact that you missed that magnificent opportunity does not mean another fine opportunity will not come again. The fact that you flopped at an interview does not mean there is no job out there for you. The fact that you have run into debt in your enterprise and facing insolvency does not mean its never going to be all right. The examinations you failed are no indication you would never pass it again. There are people who have experienced what you are going through right now, and yet they made it. They have been able to build their lives and for some, though they are dead and gone, their lives have become monumental and a point of reference to diligence, benignity and faith.

Many Failures Cannot Quench The Thirst For Success

It is very difficult to come across an individual who has had as many failures in his life as Abraham Lincoln.,[44] (United States of America's 16th president), at least among those who have memoirs or history written. He lost election many times in his bid to serve the State of Illinois Legislature and yet did not give up. The outcome was that once upon a time he had the nod and went on to be nominated for the presidential election and subsequently elected president of the country. His wife and some of his children died prematurely, and yet he did not give up hope.

A doyen in Ghanaian politics, Dr. JB Danquah is another individual whose life was filled with some amount of hurdles. 'He wrote a book on law, even before he studied the subject, and two other books before attending the University of London, though he managed to pass his matriculation exams on the third attempt'[45]. There is no successful person who is either dead or alive who was not faced with an obstacle that seems to impede him or her from building his or her life according to the plan of the supreme architect, God.

Even if you have had a very turbulent past or life as any of these alluded to above, there is one thing to recognize, that the potter would make you into another vessel. He does not give up on His clay. You can pick up where you halted. What God holds in the future for you is far more than you can imagine. Your life appeared to be marred in the hands of the potter, but you are not deserted, He needs you to know this and collaborate with him. He is already in the process of making you into another person. Accordingly, let your confession be right. Speak out from your mouth what you shall become and not what your present circumstance is. The bones may be indeed very dry, but He needs you to speak to them according to the Word of the Lord and not complain, murmur, curse or even keep describing what you see and experience.

The hand of the LORD came upon me and brought me out in the Spirit of the LORD, and set me down during the valley; Furthermore, it was full of bones. Then He caused me to pass by them all around, and behold, there were very many in the open valley; Furthermore, indeed, they were very dry. Furthermore, He said to me, "Son of man, can these bones live?" So I answered, "O Lord GOD, You know."
Again He said to me, "Prophesy to these bones, and say to them, 'O dry bones, hear the word of the LORD! Thus says the Lord GOD to these bones: "Surely I will cause breath to enter into you, and you shall live. I will put sinews on you and bring flesh upon you, cover you with skin and put breath in you; and you shall live. Then you shall know that I am the LORD."'"
So I prophesied as I was commanded; and as I prophesied, there was a noise, and suddenly a rattling; and the bones came together, bone to bone. Indeed, as I looked, the sinews and the flesh came upon them, and the skin covered them over; but there was no breath in them.
Also He said to me, "Prophesy to the breath, prophesy, son of man, and say to the breath, 'Thus says the Lord

GOD: "Come from the four winds, O breath, and breathe on these slain, that they may live."'' So I prophesied as He commanded me, and breath came into them, and they lived, and stood upon their feet, an exceedingly great army. Ezekiel 37:1-10)

You need to learn the self-discipline of confessing the Word of God even when your present circumstances and feelings appear daunting in contrast to the plan of the architect for your building. You are on the threshold of making a significant change in your life right now.

Decide to rise up and live your life again. You may be rusty, dusty and may feel you are out of date, but up to the time of death, it is not over for you.

Be An Inspiration To Others

Furthermore, when you have built your life according to the architect's plan, others can take inspiration from you to build theirs. Let someone one day say because you arose and built your life in spite of all the imminent obstacles, they will also build theirs in the face of their many adversities. This is when we would say that the life you have built has been attractive. The real beauty of life lies in its accomplishments. The paint and the finishing of your building include the scars obtained through your many battles. The contours this produces on one's life makes it unique and yours is unique indeed.

There is no builder greater than Jesus Christ is. He is our greatest inspiration. We can invite Him into our lives and apart from saving us from the wrath yet to come, He will help us build our lives. Pray this prayer with me;

Father in heaven, in the name of Jesus Christ, I humble myself and come to you to seek your grace and mercy. I ask for forgiveness for the life I have lived irreverently before coming to you. I repent of all disrespect, hypocrisy, and doubts and giving up on my life when you are ready help me.

I turn to you, Jesus, as my Lord and Personal Saviour; I completely yield the building up of my life to you. Fill me with your love not only for others but also for myself. And give me a new enthusiasm to build my life according to your plan and design. I acknowledge my need and dependency on your Spirit and ask that you fill me now.

Thank you Jesus for your abundant mercy and grace you have made available to me. For all you have already done and all you are about to do in these days and beyond, I give you all the glory now and forever more. Amen.

NOTES

[1]Daniel Aronson, Overview of Systems Thinking, Daniel Aronson is the host of the Thinking Page (http://www.thinking.net)

[2]Other examples of positive results obtained by systems thinking in service, human resources, and high-technology industries can be found in Peter Senge's classic The Fifth Discipline and in The Systems Thinker newsletter, published by Pergasus Communications.

[3]See http://www.lifeprinciples.net/whatslifeabouttext.html

[4]See Merril F. Unger's The New Unger's Bible Dictionary,R K Harrison (Editor), Howard F. Vos, Cyril J. Barber (Contributing Editors), (Chicago: Moody Press, 1988)

[5]For the full text of Dr. Martin Luther King jr speech, visit www.americanrhetoric.com/speeches/mlkihaveadream.htm

[6]See Richard Deats, Martin Luther King jr.: Spirit Led Prophet (New York: New City, 1999) pages 133 -137

[7]See Brian Tracy, Change Your Thinking, Change Your Life. (New Jersey: John Wiley & Sons, 2003) pages 3-21

[8]See Merriam-Webster Online Dictionary

[9]See John Carmody, Jeffrey Christain, Kenneth Labs, Builders Foundation Handbook, part of the National Program for Building Thermal Envelope Systems and Materials. Prepared for the US Dept of Energy, Conservation and Renewable Energy Office of Buildings and Community Systems Divisions: May 1991

[10]See www.inspect-ny.com/structure/foundationoccur.htm

[11]See John F. Walvoord, Roy B. Zuck, The Bible Knowledge Commentary (Colorado Springs: Chariot Victor Publishing, 1983) page 561

[12]See www.johnbirchalleconomist.com/developing%20value%20systems.doc: 18/08/2008

[13]http://hubpages.com/hub/SuccessfulMarriageDatingAdviceLoveIntegrityTrustRespectCommitmentGodBuildFoundation

[14]See John C. Mawell Ed., The Maxwell Leadership Bible: NKJV (Nashville: Maxwell Motivation Inc., 2002)1196 - 1197

[15]See www.statistics.gov.uk/cci/nugget.asp?id=170 "Divorces" 20/08/2008

[16]Rachael Lewis, "Things You Don't Know About Prenuptial Agreements" www.dailymail.co.uk/you/article-1033273/Things-don-8217-t-know-prenuptial-agreements.html

[17]See www.enchantedlearning.com/inventors/black.shtml ibid

[18]See www.mffordham.wordpress.com/2008/05/08/thegreatest-example-of-self-sacrifice: Bill White, paramount, California: Source: "Antonia's Mission" Readers Digest – June 2004

[19]Richard Morrison, The Anonymous Heroes Who Really Deserve A Medal at www.timesonline.co.uk/tol/comment/colunmists/richard_morrison/article4567744.(accessed 29/11/2008)

[20]Napoleon Hill, Think and Grow Rich (B N Publishing, 2007)

[21]Gladys Edmunds, "Dealing With The Minor Details Is Vital For Success" : wwww.usatoday.com/money/smallbusiness/columnists/Edmunds/2005-09-20-minor-details_x.htm

[22]Author unknown, www.itstime.com/mar99.htm

[23]See merriam-Webster Online Dictionary

[24]See merriam-Webster Online Dictionary

[26]See www.ruf.rice.edu/sch/beliefs/belief%20syllabus.htm. For Futher reading please read Gilovich, Thomas. *How We Know What Isn't So.* Free Press, 1991

[27]Pendergrast, Mark. Victims of Memory (revised edition), Upper Access, 1996

[28]Shermer, Michael. Why People Believe Weird Things, Freeman, 1997

[29]Shermer, Michael How We Believe: The Search for God in an Age of Science

[30]Charles C. Ryrie, Basic Theology, Chariot Victor Publishing, Colorado Springs, 1986; pages 210

[31]Richard L. Daft, Management (Ohio: South-Western 2003) pages 612 - 631

[32]See http://www.thefreedictionary.com/self-discipline

[33]See Kaled Asmri, The Best Success Secrets at http://successelixir. net/how-to-develop-will-power/ (accessed 20/12/2008)

[34]See Steve Pavalina, Personal Development for Smart People. http:// www.stevepavlina.com/blog/2005/06/self-discipline-willpower/ (accessed 20 /06/2005)

[35]http://www.brainyquote.com/quotes/quotes/h/henrywad-sw129800.html

[36]See Jack Canfield, Janet Switzer, The Success Principles (London: Harper Collins, 2005) page 189 -269

[37]See Philip Kotler, Marketing Manager (New Jersey: Pearson Education, 2003) page 76

[38]See www.theodore-roosevelt.com/trsorbonnespeech.html

[39]Myles Munroe, Spirit of Leadership (New Kensington: Whitaker House, 2004) page 207

[40]See Winston Churchill, ed. Never Give In!: The Best of Winston Churchill's Speeches (New York: Hyerion, 2003) page xxviii

[41]Robert Frank, The Wealth Report, The Wall Street Journal (http:// blogs.wsj.com/wealth/2008/01/14/the-decline-of-inherited-money/

[42]David Yukelson, PhD, Coordinator of Sport Psychology Services Morgan Academic Support Centre for Student-Atletics, Penn State University. "What is Mental Toughness and How To Develop It" www. mascsa.psu.edu/dave/Mental-Toughness.pdf : 20/03/2004

[43]see http://www.merriam-webster.com/dictionary/time

[44]See history of Galileo Galilei, http://en.wikipedia.org/wiki/Galileo_Galilei (accessed 13/01/07)

[45]Robert Guest, "The Shackled Continent: Africa's Past, Present and Future" (Oxford: Pan Books, 2004) pages 108-138

[46]Janet A. Simons, Donald B. Irwin and Beverly A. Drinnien, The Search for Understanding, West Publishing Company, New York, 1987

[47]See the life of Abraham Lincoln: 1637 - Samuel Lincoln from Hingham, England settles in Hingham, Massachusetts.

1778 - Thomas Lincoln (Abraham's father), descendant of Samuel, is born in Virginia.

1782 - Thomas and family move to Kentucky.

1786 - Thomas' father is killed by Native Americans.

1806 - Thomas marries Nancy Hanks. A daughter, Sarah is born eight months later.

1808 - Thomas buys a farm called Sinking Spring near Hodgenville, Kentucky.

Feb. 12, 1809 - Abraham Lincoln is born in a one room log cabin on Nolin Creek in Kentucky.

1811 - In Spring, the Lincoln family moves to a 230 acre farm on Knob Creek ten miles from Sinking Spring.

1812 - A brother, Thomas, is born but dies in infancy.

1815 - Young Abraham attends a log school house.

1816 - Briefly attends school. In December, the Lincoln family crosses the Ohio River and settles in the backwoods of Indiana.

1817 - In February, Abraham, age 7, shoots a wild turkey but suffers great remorse and never hunts game again.

1818 - Young Abraham is kicked in the head by a horse and for a brief time is thought to be dead. Oct. 5, Nancy Hanks Lincoln (his mother) dies of "milk sickness."

1819 - On Dec. 2, Abraham's father, Thomas, marries a widow, Sarah Bush Johnston, and becomes stepfather to her three children. Abraham develops much affection for his stepmother.

1820 - Briefly attends school.

1822 - Attends school for a few months.

1824 - Does plowing and planting and work for hire for neighbours. Attends school in the fall and winter. Borrows books and reads whenever possible.

1828 - On Jan. 20, his married sister Sarah dies while giving birth. In April, Abraham, now 19, and Allen Gentry take a flatboat of cargo of farm produce to New Orleans. During the trip they fight off an robbery attack by seven black men. At New Orleans Abe observes a slave auction.

1830 - In March, Abe and his family begin a 200 mile journey to move to Illinois where they settle on uncleared land along the Sangamon River, near Decatur. Abe makes his first political speech in favor of improving navigation on the Sangamon River.

1831 - Abe makes a second flatboat trip to New Orleans. His father moves again, but Abe doesn't go and instead settles in New Salem, Illinois, where he works as a clerk in the village store and sleeps in the back. Wrestles a man named Jack Armstrong to a draw. Learns basic math, reads Shakespeare and Robert Burns and participates in a local debating society.

1832 - In March, becomes a candidate for Illinois General Assembly. The Black Hawk War breaks out. In April, Abe enlists and is elected Captain of his rifle company. Re-enlists as a private after company is disbanded. He serves a total of three months but does not fight in a battle. August 6, loses the election. The village store he worked in goes out of business. Lincoln and partner, William Berry, purchase another village store in New Salem.

1833 - The store fails, leaving him badly in debt. Lincoln is appointed Postmaster of New Salem. In Autumn, Lincoln is appointed Deputy County Surveyor.

1834 - On August 4, Lincoln, age 24, is elected to the Illinois General Assembly as a member of the Whig party. Begins to study law. In December, meets Stephen A. Douglas, 21, a Democrat.

1835 - In January, former store partner William Berry dies, increasing Lincoln's debt to $1000. On August 25, Ann Rutledge, Lincoln's love interest, dies from fever at age 22.

1836 - August 1, re-elected to the Illinois Gen. Assembly and by now is a leader of the Whig party. September 9, Lincoln receives his law license. Begins courtship of Mary Owens, 28. Has an episode of severe depression in December.

1837 - Helps to get the Illinois state capital moved from Vandalia to Springfield. April 15, leaves New Salem and settles in Springfield. Becomes a law partner of John T. Stuart. In Summer, proposes marriage to Mary Owens, is turned down and the courtship ends.

1838 - Helps to successfully defend Henry Truett in a famous murder case. August 6, re-elected to the Illinois Gen. Assembly, becoming Whig floor leader.

1839 - Travels through nine counties in central and eastern Illinois as a lawyer on the 8th Judicial Circuit. December 3, admitted to practice in United States Circuit Court. Meets Mary Todd, 21, at a dance.

1840 - In June, Lincoln argues his first case before the Illinois Supreme Court. August 3, re-elected to the Illinois Gen. Assembly. In Fall, becomes engaged to Mary Todd.

1841 - January 1, breaks off engagement with Mary Todd. Has episode of depression. March 1, forms new law partnership with Stephen T. Logan. In August, makes a trip by steamboat to Kentucky and sees twelve slaves chained together.

1842 - Does not seek re-election to the legislature. In Summer, resumes courtship with Mary Todd. In September, accepts a challenge to a duel by Democratic state auditor James Shields over published letters making fun of Shields. September 22, duel with swords is averted by an explanation of letters. November 4, marries Mary Todd in Springfield.

1843 - Lincoln is unsuccessful in try for the Whig nomination for U.S. Congress. August 1, first child, Robert Todd Lincoln, is born.

1844 - May, the Lincoln family moves into a house in Springfield, bought for $1500. Campaigns for Henry Clay in the presidential election. In December, dissolves law partnership with Logan, then sets up his own practice.

1846 - March 10, a son, Edward Baker Lincoln is born. May 1, nominated to be the Whig candidate for U.S. Congress. August 3, elected to the U.S. House of Representatives.

1847 - Moves into a boarding house in Washington, D.C. with his wife and sons. December 6, takes his seat when Thirtieth Congress convenes. December 22, presents resolutions questioning President Polk about U.S. hostilities with Mexico.

1848 - January 22, gives a speech on floor of the House against President Polk's war policy regarding Mexico. In June, attends the national Whig convention supporting General Zachary Taylor as the nominee for president. Campaigns for Taylor in Maryland and in Boston, Mass., then in Illinois.

1849 - March 7 and 8, makes an appeal before the U.S. Supreme Court regarding the Illinois statute of limitations, but is unsuccessful. March 31, returns to Springfield and leaves politics to practice law. On May 22, Abraham Lincoln is granted U.S. Patent No. 6,469 (the only president ever granted a patent).

1850 - February 1, his son Edward dies after a two month illness. Lincoln resumes his travels in the 8th Judicial Circuit covering over 400 miles in 14 counties in Illinois. 'Honest Abe' gains a reputation as an outstanding lawyer. December 21, his third son, William Wallace Lincoln (Willie) is born.

1851 - January 17, Lincoln's father dies.

1853 - April 4, his fourth son, Thomas (Tad) is born.

1854 - Re-enters politics opposing the <u>Kansas-Nebraska Act</u>. Elected to Illinois legislature but declines the seat in order to try to become U.S. Senator.

1855 - Does not get chosen by the Illinois legislature to be U.S. Senator.

1856 - May 29, helps organize the new Republican party of Illinois. At the first Republican convention Lincoln gets 110 votes for the vice-presidential nomination, bringing him national attention. Campaigns in Illinois for Republican presidential candidate, John C. Frémont.

1857 - June 26, in Springfield, Lincoln speaks against the <u>Dred Scott decision.</u>

1858 - In May, wins acquittal in a murder trial by using an almanac regarding the height of the moon to discredit a witness. June 16, nominated to be the Republican senator from Illinois, opposing Democrat <u>Stephen A. Douglas</u>. Gives <u>"House Divided" speech</u> at the state convention in Springfield. Also engages Douglas in a series of seven debates with big audiences.

1859 - Illinois legislature chooses Douglas for the U.S. Senate over Lincoln by a vote of 54 to 46. In the Fall, Lincoln makes his last trip through the 8th Judicial Circuit. December 20, writes a short <u>autobiography.</u>

1860 - March 6, delivers an impassioned political <u>speech on slavery</u> in New Haven, Connecticut. Also in March, the 'Lincoln-Douglas Debates' published.

May 18, 1860 - Nominated to be the Republican candidate for President of the United States. Opposes Northern Democrat Stephen A. Douglas and Southern Democrat John C. Breckinridge. In June, writes a <u>longer autobiography.</u>

November 6, 1860 - Abraham Lincoln is elected as 16th U.S. president and the first Republican. Receives 180 of 303 possible electoral votes and 40 percent of the popular vote.

Dec 20, 1860 - South Carolina secedes from the Union. Followed within two months by Mississippi, Florida, Alabama, Georgia, Louisiana and Texas.

Feb 11, 1861 - Lincoln gives a brief <u>farewell</u> to friends and supporters at Springfield and leaves by train for Washington. Receives a warning during the trip about a possible assassination attempt.

March 4, 1861 - Inauguration ceremonies in Washington. President Lincoln delivers his <u>First Inaugural Address.</u>

April 12, 1861 - At 4:30 a.m. Confederates open fire on Fort Sumter in Charleston. The Civil War begins.

April 15, 1861 - President Lincoln issues a <u>Proclamation Calling Militia and Convening Congress.</u>

April 17, 1861 - Virginia secedes from the Union. Followed within five weeks by North Carolina, Tennessee and Arkansas, thus forming an eleven state Confederacy.

April 19, 1861 - The president issues a <u>Proclaimation of Blockade</u> against Southern ports.

April 27, 1861 - The president authorizes the suspension of the Writ of Habeas Corpus.

June 3, 1861 - Political rival Stephen A. Douglas dies unexpectedly of acute rheumatism.

July 21, 1861 - The Union suffers a defeat at <u>Bull Run</u> in northern Virginia. Union troops fall back to Washington. The president realizes the war will be long.

July 27, 1861 - Appoints George B. <u>McClellan</u> as commander of the Department of the Potomac.

Aug 6, 1861 - Signs a law freeing slaves being used by the Confederates in their war effort.

Aug 12, 1861 - The president issues a <u>Proclamation of a National Day of Fasting.</u>

Sept 11, 1861 - Revokes Gen. John C. Frémont's unauthorized military proclamation of emancipation in Missouri.

Oct 24, 1861 - Relieves Gen. Frémont of his command and replaces him with Gen. David Hunter.

Nov 1, 1861 - Appoints McClellan as commander of the Union army after the resignation of Winfield <u>Scott.</u>

Jan 27, 1862 - Issues <u>General War Order No. 1</u> calling for a Union advance to begin Feb 22.

Feb 3, 1862 - Writes a <u>message to McClellan</u> on a difference of opinion regarding military plans.

Feb 20, 1862 - The president's son Willie dies at age 11. The <u>president's wife</u> is emotionally devastated and never fully recovers.

March 11, 1862 - President Lincoln relieves McClellan as general-in-chief and takes direct command of the Union armies.

April 6, 1862 - Confederate surprise attack on Gen. Ulysses S. Grant's troops at Shiloh on the Tennessee River results in a bitter struggle with 13,000 Union killed and wounded and 10,000 Confederates. The president is then pressured to relieve Grant but resists.

April 9, 1862 - Writes a message to McClellan urging him to attack.

April 16, 1862 - Signs an Act abolishing slavery in the District of Columbia.

May 20, 1862 - Approves the Federal Homestead Law giving 160 acres of publicly owned land to anyone who will claim and then work the property for 5 years. Thousands then cross the Mississippi to tame the 'Wild West.'

June 19, 1862 - Approves a Law prohibiting slavery in the territories.

Aug 29/30, 1862 - Union defeat at the second Battle of Bull Run in northern Virginia. The Union Army retreats to Washington. The president then relieves Union commander Gen. John Pope.

Sept 17, 1862 - General Robert E. Lee and the Confederate armies are stopped at Antietam in Maryland by McClellan and numerically superior Union forces. By nightfall, 26,000 men are dead, wounded or missing - the bloodiest day in U.S. military history.

Sept 22, 1862 - The president issues a preliminary Emancipation Proclamation freeing the slaves.

Nov 5, 1862 - The president names Ambrose E. Burnside as commander of the Army of the Potomac, replacing McClellan.

Dec 13, 1862 - Army of the Potomac suffers a costly defeat at Fredericksburg in Virginia with a loss of 12,653 men. Confederate losses are 5,309.

Dec 22, 1862 - The president writes a brief message to the Army of the Potomac.

Dec 31, 1862 - The president signs a bill admitting West Virginia to the Union.

Jan 1, 1863 - President Lincoln issues the final Emancipation Proclamation freeing all slaves in territories held by Confederates. **Page one of the Document**

Jan 25, 1863 - The president appoints Joseph (Fighting Joe) Hooker as commander of the Army of the Potomac, replacing Burnside.

Jan 26, 1863 - Writes a message to Hooker.

Jan 29, 1863 - Gen. Grant is placed in command of the Army of the West, with orders to capture Vicksburg.

Feb 25, 1863 - Signs a Bill creating a national banking system.

March 3, 1863 - Signs an Act introducing military conscription.

May 1-4, 1863 - A Union defeat at the Battle of Chancellorsville in Virginia. Confederate Gen. Stonewall Jackson is mortally wounded. Hooker retreats. Union losses are 17,000 killed, wounded and missing. The Confederates, 13, 000.

June 28, 1863 - The president appoints George G. Meade as commander of the Army of the Potomac, replacing Hooker.

July 3, 1863 - Confederate defeat at the Battle of Gettysburg.

July 4, 1863 - Vicksburg, the last Confederate stronghold on the Mississippi, is captured by the Gen. Grant and the Army of the West.

July 13, 1863 - Writes a message to Grant.

July 14, 1863 - Writes an undelivered letter to Meade complaining about his failure to capture Lee.

July 30, 1863 - Issues an Order of Retaliation.

Aug 8, 1863 - Writes a letter to his wife regarding Tad's lost goat.

Aug 10, 1863 - The president meets with abolitionist Frederick Douglass who pushes for full equality for Union 'Negro troops.'

Sept 19/20, 1863 - Union defeat at Chickamauga in Georgia leaves Chattanooga in Tennessee under Confederate siege. The president appoints Gen. Grant to command all operations in the western theater.

Oct 3, 1863 - Issues a Proclamation of Thanksgiving.

Nov 19, 1863 - President Lincoln delivers the Gettysburg Address at a ceremony dedicating the Battlefield as a national cemetery.

Dec 8, 1863 - The president issues a Proclamation of Amnesty and Reconstruction for restoration of the Union.

March 12, 1864 - President Lincoln appoints Grant as general-in-chief of all the Federal armies. William T. Sherman succeeds Grant as commander in the West.

June 3, 1864 - A costly mistake by Grant results in 7,000 Union casualties in twenty minutes during an offensive against entrenched Rebels at Cold Harbor, Virginia.

June 8, 1864 - Abraham Lincoln is nominated for president by a coalition of Republicans and War Democrats.

July 18, 1864 - Issues a call for 500,000 Volunteers for military service.

Aug 31, 1864 - Makes a speech to 148th Ohio Regiment.

Sept 2, 1864 - Atlanta is captured by Sherman's army. Later, the president on advice from Grant approves Sherman's march to the sea.

Oct 19, 1864 - A decisive Union victory by Gen. Philip H. Sheridan in the Shenandoah Valley.

Nov 8, 1864 - Abraham Lincoln is re-elected president, defeating Democrat George B. McClellan. Lincoln gets 212 of 233 electoral votes and 55 percent of the popular vote.

Dec 20, 1864 - Sherman reaches Savannah in Georgia leaving behind a path of destruction 60 miles wide all the way from Atlanta.

March 4, 1865 - Inauguration ceremonies in Washington. President Lincoln delivers his second Inaugural Address.

March 17, 1865 - A kidnap plot by John Wilkes Booth fails when Lincoln fails to arrive as expected at the Soldiers' Home.

April 9, 1865 - Gen. Robert E. Lee surrenders his Confederate army to Gen. Ulysses S. Grant at the village of Appomattox Court House in Virginia.

April 10, 1865 - Celebrations break out in Washington.

April 11, 1865 - President Lincoln makes his last public speech, which focuses on the problems of reconstruction. The United States flag 'Stars and Stripes' is raised over Fort Sumter.

April 14, 1865 - Lincoln and his wife Mary see the play "Our American Cousin" at Ford's Theater. About 10:13 p.m., during the third act of the play, John Wilkes Booth shoots the president in the head. Doctors attend to the president in the theater then move him to a house across the street. He never regains consciousness.

April 15, 1865 - President Abraham Lincoln dies at 7:22 in the morning.

April 26, 1865 - John Wilkes Booth is shot and killed in a tobacco barn in Virginia.

May 4, 1865 - Abraham Lincoln is laid to rest in Oak Ridge Cemetery, outside Springfield, Illinois.

Dec 6, 1865 - The Thirteenth Amendment to the United States Constitution, passed by Congress on January 31, 1865, is finally ratified. Slavery is abolished.

The Archives of Mr V O D Twum-Barima, Dr. J B Danquah, Ghana's President We Never Had (Part 1) www.http://www.thestatesmanon-line.com/pages/news_detail.php?newsid=2063&section=7 30/09/08

www.ingramcontent.com/pod-product-compliance
Lightning Source LLC
Chambersburg PA
CBHW062155120626
46550CB00012B/1581